Helping Gay Men Find Love

Helping Gay Men Find Love

**TIPS FOR GUYS ON DATING AND BEGINNING
A HEALTHY RELATIONSHIP**

Israel Martinez

© 2017 Israel Martinez
All rights reserved.

ISBN-13: 9781546560197
ISBN-10: 154656019X

For my husband, Matt—a life partner who continues to exceed my wildest expectations

Contents

Introduction · **xiii**

Chapter 1 **Accept Being Single for the Moment** · · · · · · · · · · · · · · · · **1**

    Beware of Desperation: It Clouds Your Thinking · · · · · · · · · 2

    Making Informed Decisions · 3

    The Power of Loneliness · 3

    The Power of Acceptance · 4

    Are You Able to Accept Being Single for the Moment? (Quiz) · 5

    Your True Love Story: Being Comfortable While Single Can Lead to a Lifetime of Love · · · · · · · · · · · · 6

    References · 7

Chapter 2	**Thorough Assessment of Self** ······················ **8**
	Why Our Self-Esteem May Take a Hit ···················· 8
	Discover Your Strengths ································· 9
	Own Your Strengths ····································10
	Is Your Self-Esteem Where It Needs to Be? (Quiz) ········11
	Your True Love Story: The Work Starts with the Self ····11
	References ··13
Chapter 3	**Figure out Your True Needs** ······················ **14**
	Look Out for the Parent Trap ···························14
	Are You Really Only into Masculine Guys? ···············15
	Do Not Go to Extremes ·································16
	What Really Matters ···································16
	Do You Know Which Traits Matter? (Quiz) ··············17
	Your True Love Story: What Matters Most ··············18
	Reference ···20
	Traits That Matter (Work Sheet) ·······················20

Chapter 4 **Make Use of Past Relationships** ··················· **23**

    Every Relationship Deserves Some Grieving ············23

    How to Give Your Feelings the Attention
They Deserve···24

    When You Are Done, Make Sure You Are Done·········25

    Learn from Experience ····································27

    A Relationship Ending Does Not Equal Failure ··········28

    Are You Ready to Move On? (Quiz) ·····················29

    Your True Love Story: Dealing with the Past before
Moving On to the Future ··································30

    Reference···31

Chapter 5 **Decide How to Meet**······························ **32**

    The Truth about the Bar Scene ··························33

    Hook-Up Apps Are for Hooking Up ·····················35

    Online Dating Sites Are Worth a Try·····················35

    That's What Friends Are For······························37

    Do What You Like ··37

How to Approach Your Prospects··················39

Do You Know How to Best Meet the Man of Your
Dreams? (Quiz)··42

Your True Love Story: Online Leading to In Love········42

Interests (Work Sheet)··································45

Chapter 6 **Have the Best First Date** ························**46**

Picking the Perfect Place······························46

It's Not You; It's Him··································48

How to Wrap Things Up·······························49

Sex on the First Date?··································50

Should There Be a Second Date? (Quiz)················52

Your True Love Story: Keeping That First-Date Feeling··53

Reference··54

Chapter 7 **Keep the Dating Momentum Going**················**55**

Be More Adventurous and More Relaxed···············55

Bring in the Friends····································56

Meet the Parents · 58

Your First Argument · 60

Thriving Past Date One (Quiz) · 62

Your True Love Story: The Importance of
Family—Warts and All · 63

Reference · 66

Chapter 8 Sex—Let's Talk about It · 67

Let's Get the Sexually Transmitted Infections (STI)
Talk out of the Way · 67

To Be or Not to Be...Monogamous · 69

How to Have Mind-Blowing Sex · 70

Grooming · 72

Love the Skin You're In · 73

Are You Ready for Hot Sex? (Quiz) · 74

Your True Love Story: When It Comes to Sex,
Let It All Hang Out · 75

References · 77

Chapter 9	**Things Are Getting Serious**	78
	Just the Toothbrush?	78
	Handling Disagreements	79
	Moving In	81
	Pop the Question?	86
	Could This Be What I Was Looking For? (Quiz)	87
	Your True Love Story: Talk Like Your Love Depends on It	88
	References	90
Chapter 10	**Final Words of Advice and Encouragement**	91
	References	**95**

Introduction

I care about you. I want you to meet the man of your dreams and have that turn into a healthy and satisfying relationship that makes you feel at peace, relaxed, and challenged by your partner to tap into your strengths and be a more fully realized self. This is a great place to get to, yet the road there could be extremely difficult. This book will take away the roadblocks so that you're more likely to meet a guy who is a great fit for you.

If you are still reading this, you understand that entering a healthy relationship is not easy and that you could use some help. You realize that finding a partner involves making wise choices and stepping out of your comfort zone just enough to allow for something different, something better, to happen in your life. If you truly want to be in a fulfilling relationship and are willing to do the work, then this book is worth your time, money, and energy (TME). Throughout this book, I will be referring to your TME, because as I said, I care about you and want to make sure you don't waste your TME; it's precious, and so are you.

Did I just call you precious? Yes. Do I really believe that without having met you? Yes. I'm confident that if you are picking up this book to get an assist in being in a healthy relationship, you are one of the good guys. I know you are open to learning and growing in order to have positive things happen in your life. I also know that as a gay man, you likely had to go through some struggles (I sure did), and you have made it to this point where you feel ready to begin a journey toward a fulfilling relationship. I admire that strength and determination. You are precious.

Please allow me to tell you why I wrote this book and how you will get the most out of it. Our community needs a book like this because, for many reasons, it's more difficult for gay men to enter into and maintain healthy relationships compared to our heterosexual counterparts. Let's start off with a statistical fact: we have fewer options. There are fewer men for a gay man to choose from than women for a heterosexual man to choose from. This handicap is worsened by the fact that we cannot always tell which men we actually are able to choose from—meaning that because of the stigmas still present in society and the lack of clear identifying features, we may not know who is actually gay. From our workplaces to the grocery store, we just may not know who is on our team and a possible match.

Once we figure out who is gay and an option for us, there are still elements of the gay culture, biology, and society's narrow-mindedness that make it difficult for us to keep healthy relationships. As men, we tend to be fine with one-night stands; it's in our evolutionary best interest to not be so discerning about how many people with whom we have sex. I would say that gay culture has embraced the one-night stand as fun, acceptable, and sometimes an accomplishment. As you will learn later in this book, while possibly fun, one-night stands have the ability to get in the way of entering a healthy relationship. Also, within our culture, even with the advent of national gay-marriage rights, there are fewer expectations than in the heterosexual realm of couples staying together long-term. I have often heard the joke that one year together for a gay couple is like seven for a straight couple.

This way of thinking about gay couples is not exclusive to gay men. It's not uncommon for heterosexual friends and family members to not see a gay couple as a unit that should be celebrated and supported. This lack of acknowledgment can make it easier for that couple to just throw in the towel when their relationship experiences difficult times instead of working through issues. Lastly, gay men do tend to struggle to be vulnerable with other men in general. This makes sense when you consider that many of us hid our identities from others—especially our male friends while growing up—because we wanted to fit in and have friends or, at the very least, not be bullied and beat up. Now all of sudden, as adults, are we supposed to just let go of so many years of hiding ourselves from other men and bare our souls to our boyfriends or husbands? This is not an easy thing to do.

Even with these additional roadblocks, I promise you that a healthy relationship is a realistic option for you. Just keep reading. Let me explain now why you should trust what I have to say in this book.

I became a psychotherapist to give people in my community—the lesbian, gay, bisexual, transgender (LGBT) community—the opportunity to work on their mental health in an environment that was safe and comfortable and with a professional who had researched, trained, and experienced what it's like to be part of the LGBT community. Within my expertise, I'm especially proficient in the experiences of gay men.

My passion is to provide gay men with as many tools and advantages as possible to help them live more authentic and fulfilled lives. Through my private practice, I'm only able to reach so many people. This book is my attempt to provide more gay men with an opportunity to feel truly understood as I guide them through self-discovery and love. It's also my attempt to even up the score a bit and allow gay men access to information and advice that is relevant to our actual experiences. Most of the advice out there is created by and for a heterosexual population, so it does not speak fully to whom we are and should not be our only option.

I also wrote this book because I know what I'm talking about. Not only am I a gay male psychotherapist who has researched, trained, and experienced gay life, but I also treat gay men on issues specific to romantic relationships, and—for some of you, this may be the most important credential—I have used the techniques I offer in this book to get me where I'm today: in an extremely fulfilling, nurturing, and loving relationship with my husband.

To help with your journey toward this same goal, let me share the best way for you to make use of this book. It's important that you read each chapter in order, as the skills and advice build off all of the previous skills and advice. You will also get more out of each of the activities suggested if you really commit to completing them. This means taking the recommended time mentioned to complete each one and revisiting the exercise a day or two after initially working on it so that your brain is coming at it with a fresh perspective. This new way of looking at the activity will allow you to include pieces of information that you might have missed and that could prove vital to figuring out how you will land your match and begin your healthy relationship.

You will also find useful checklists at the end of each main chapter. Carefully considering each item in a checklist will allow you to know if you have absorbed and followed through with what was needed or if you need to spend more time working on certain goals. As with the activities in this book, you do not want to speed through these checklists. They will let you know if you are truly ready to move on.

After each chapter, you will find a true love story of a gay couple. I provided these case studies to give real-life support for the tips offered in this book and to give hope that healthy, loving, and fulfilling relationships are definitely a possibility if you are smart about how you pursue them. While the stories are true, I have changed each person's name in order to protect his privacy.

Let's get started!

CHAPTER 1
Accept Being Single for the Moment

Remember, I care about your TME (time, money, and energy). To help not waste your TME, we have to begin our process of finding your relationship match by doing some work before we actually start heading out and looking for "the one." Think of it as being smart about what you pack and how you prepare for your journey in order to ensure that you have all you need and are able to have a successful experience.

Before the work of looking happens, you need to make sure that you are in a place that will actually allow you to make good decisions about who is worthy of being your partner. This is a fundamental building block toward being able to enter a healthy relationship. Some may ask, "If you can't love yourself, how are you going to be able to love somebody else?" Let's start by making sure you know you are as precious as I think you are.

The upcoming chapters on what to do before you start looking will help you avoid being, and therefore seeming, desperate to be in a relationship.

As you can imagine, this is not attractive and will guarantee that you make poor decisions and waste your TME. The chapters in this section will also help you better understand the value you offer to others and that you are as great as others see you.

Feeling comfortable with your single status is key to entering a healthy relationship. Sound like a paradox? Read on, and you will understand why this works.

Beware of Desperation: It Clouds Your Thinking

If you have ever gone to the grocery store when you are hungry, you know it's usually a recipe for disaster. Instead of making decisions with your head or wallet, you think with your stomach. Unfortunately, your stomach does not care about your budget, the weight you are trying to maintain or lose, or the fact that you hated a particular snack last time you bought it.

A similar phenomenon happens if you go out desperately looking to find "the one," and you expend most of your energy scouring the crowds for Mr. Right. When you are that starved for love, your judgment becomes easily compromised. You may wind up connecting with people you know would not interest you if you were not so "hungry," and then you bring home an unsatisfying "snack." We have all been there. I know I've brought home my share of guys I should have just left on the shelf.

If you accept being single *for the moment*, you give yourself the freedom to make more informed decisions about who is worth the investment of your TME—and who is not. We all have limited personal resources, so it's important to use them where we will gain the most benefit. Accepting your single status enables you to avoid clinging to someone who is a bad match for the sake of being in a relationship and then struggling to figure out if the relationship is a keeper or not.

Making Informed Decisions

It's best to make wise decisions when first meeting a potential mate—before you find yourself stuck in the momentum of the relationship. Making uninformed decisions makes it likely that you will enter a relationship that isn't optimal or is downright unhealthy for you. Once we're already in relationships, we can easily get caught up and stay in them for the wrong reasons. And the longer it goes on, the harder it is to change directions. The best way to avoid this huge waste of TME is to make better decisions from the beginning.

To make wiser decisions, you cannot have your brain clouded by desperation to avoid being alone; instead, you need some level of comfort being on your own. How many times have we stayed in relationships, experienced unnecessary pain, and endured unhappiness just so we could escape feeling alone? The fear of loneliness often deters us from making and following through with wise decisions. If we accept being single, then that fear of loneliness loses its power over us.

The Power of Loneliness

Gay men are especially susceptible to the emotional stress that comes with fears of loneliness. This is due partly because most gay men experience some level of internalized homophobia, and this serves to lower our comfort levels for being on our own. Because of the abundance of negative words, images, and connections put out there by friends, family, media, and society, we cannot help but take some of that in and mistakenly believe we are bad or negative people. The degree to which we experience feelings of internalized homophobia plays a role in determining how well we are able to love ourselves and how secure we are with ourselves (Weber 2008). The more we love and believe in ourselves, the less love and validation we need from others in order to feel whole.

Another reason we are more vulnerable to loneliness is the lack of support we received growing up versus that of our heterosexual peers. Evidence shows that gay men tend to have less support available to them when young (Friedman, Marshal, Stall, Cheong, and Wright 2008) because (1) we are more likely to isolate ourselves due to the shame or confusion we felt for being different than our peers; (2) we might have felt unsafe getting close to others, especially men, because we did not want them to learn of our sexual orientation; or (3) others might have shunned us because of their limited and negative beliefs regarding homosexuality. Any of these reasons would negatively affect us, making it more difficult for us to feel comfortable being on our own.

The Power of Acceptance

In order to help us accept being single—despite feeling like we are actually "starving" to be in a relationship—we must change the way we view our reality. How is that possible? With *radical acceptance*. Radical acceptance occurs when we fully (or radically) accept those things we cannot control. At various points in our lives, we have probably practiced this technique. In fact, we employ radical acceptance every time we relinquish control of a situation's outcome, knowing there is nothing we can do to affect it. It doesn't mean we become complacent and give up; instead, it means we acknowledge our inability to manipulate a situation to go exactly the way we would like.

One way to accomplish radical acceptance is through self-talk. We actually tell ourselves, out loud or internally, that whether or not tonight is the night we meet our significant other is out of our control. While there are things we are able to do that will increase our chances of entering a healthy relationship—like accepting being single for the moment—there are still a lot of variables beyond our control. If we radically accept this and focus our energy on something more productive, such as living in the moment and enjoying ourselves and our friends when out, we will be happier individuals and make more informed decisions when it comes time to enter a relationship. We all know that being on the prowl is not a cute look. Just relax, and enjoy yourself.

Are You Able to Accept Being Single for the Moment? (Quiz)

When you've given radical acceptance some time and practice, use the checklist below to see if you have made some progress in your efforts to accept being single for the moment. If you have more checked than empty boxes, then you're definitely heading in the right direction to begin a healthy relationship. If you have more empty boxes, spend further time with the tips in this chapter, focusing on yourself.

- ☐ When I go out with friends, I'm focused on enjoying their company.
- ☐ If I do not meet a potential date when out, I do not beat myself up over it.

- ☐ I can watch or read a love story or listen to a love song without asking myself a million times why I'm not in a relationship.
- ☐ I enjoy spending some time on my own.
- ☐ If a date does not go well, I'm not still hoping that the person will call me.
- ☐ If I meet someone and have a pretty good idea he is not right for me, I do not pursue dating him "just to see where it goes."
- ☐ I check my dating-site profiles or apps only twice a day (if applicable).

Your True Love Story: Being Comfortable While Single Can Lead to a Lifetime of Love

Matthew (sixty-four) and Martin (sixty-one)

Together: thirty-five years

When Matthew and Martin first met, Matthew was definitely not looking to be in a relationship. He had moved to a big city two years prior and was finishing his master's, working, and enjoying the gay nightlife. A year earlier he had come out of a six-year, unhealthy relationship.

As part of enjoying the gay nightlife, and not on the prowl to meet his perfect mate, he would frequent a bar that he felt was "clean cut" and sort of "preppy." One night in 1981, Matthew met Martin. They have different versions of who picked up whom, but regardless, Matthew's lack of desperation to be in a relationship allowed him to be available for Martin, who seemed to be a potential match.

Matthew decided to give dating Martin a chance and found that this relationship was going well and running very smoothly. His needs were met, and Martin wasn't just serving as a body to have around so that Matthew wasn't lonely. Six months after they started dating, they felt confident enough in their relationship to decide to live together. For them, it felt as if moving in together was the most natural next step in order to take their relationship to the next level. Even with this strong feeling about the two of them, Matthew admits that he did have a small case of cold feet. He feels he did not doubt the strength of the relationship; he just wanted to be completely sure that they were doing the right thing. And almost immediately after moving in together, they both felt that they had made the right decision.

Over thirty years later, they still enjoy living and being together. What they appreciate most about their relationship is the humor, companionship, and support they consistently provide for each other. They are also grateful that they were discerning about their relationship from the beginning; because of that, they have had the pleasure of sharing experiences with each other, good and bad, throughout the years.

References

Friedman, M. S., M. P. Marshal, R. Stall, J. Cheong, and E. R. Wright. 2008. "Gay-related Development, Early Abuse and Adult Health Outcomes Among Gay Males." *AIDS and Behavior* 12: 891–902.

Weber, G. N. 2008. "Using to Numb the Pain: Substance Use and Abuse Among Lesbian, Gay, and Bisexual Individuals." *Journal of Mental Health Counseling* 30 (1): 31–48.

CHAPTER 2
Thorough Assessment of Self

When we think about entering relationships, we tend to focus on the qualities we are looking for in a potential partner. Sometimes we become so fixated on the traits we want that we lose sight of all of the amazing qualities we have to offer. If we don't acknowledge our own attributes, we handicap our chances of entering healthy relationships in two ways: (1) we do not present our truest, best selves, and (2) we end up settling, believing we do not deserve more.

Why Our Self-Esteem May Take a Hit
As gay men, we have a greater tendency than our heterosexual counterparts to play down our strengths. This does not mean we are less worthy. It just means that because we have endured issues that affected the development of who we are while growing up, our self-esteem might have taken a hit.

Self-acceptance is key to our mental and emotional health; however, societal homophobia and heterosexism have been shown to interfere with the development of self-acceptance (Weber-Gilmore, Rose, and

Rubinstein 2011). Since we are continuously bombarded with messages geared to a heterosexual population—be they advertisements, movies, jokes, or religion—the development of our own healthy identities may be thwarted since it becomes more difficult to be OK with ourselves when so much out there is telling us that we're not "normal." Further compounding the issue is the outright rejection of our sexual-minority status through homophobic images and messaging.

In addition, unlike other minority groups (such as Hispanics and African Americans), we likely did not grow up in families or communities that shared, embraced, and supported our sexual orientation (Morrow 2004). For example, if teased at school about being gay, most of us did not return home to gay parents or siblings who would help us take pride in this difference and incorporate it into our identities. Instead, we lived with hidden shame that allowed us to feel bad about ourselves.

Discover Your Strengths

While these obstacles have gotten in the way of a more accurate sense of self and self-esteem for many of us, they have also created unique strengths that some of us may not even be aware of. I have heard many successful gay men speak to being gay as a part of themselves that allowed them to achieve great things. For example, many of us had to struggle through life to protect ourselves from being harmed physically and emotionally because we were seen by certain people as weak since we were not as masculine as other boys. This struggle helped us to learn survival skills that we could then apply to our personal and professional lives in order to succeed. Getting through such adversity has also helped many gay men be empathetic toward and inclusive of others. These are great attributes to have and should be realized and celebrated.

How do we get a better sense of our strengths? We begin by making a list of our positive qualities—first by asking ourselves what our attributes are and then by asking our friends and family members what they observe to be our strengths. It's important to also gather insight from our friends and family. If we rely solely on our own observations, we'll likely sell ourselves short either because we simply do not see our gifts, or we are too shy or insecure to acknowledge them.

Own Your Strengths
Next, you must actually *believe* everything you have listed. A simple exercise for realizing how great you truly are is this: for each trait you have trouble accepting, write that trait on the top of a sheet of paper and learn to "own" it. For example, "I am kind." Under that attribute, create two columns—one that says "Evidence For" and the other labeled "Evidence Against." Then fill out each column. Be objective here; do not allow self-doubt to detract from the positive evidence. Revisit this exercise the day after initially working on it, and see what else you are able to add. A new day will provide fresh perspective and new evidence.

When we examine what we have written, our strengths should become more obvious to us. We will often find that we were not allowing ourselves to fully appreciate our positive qualities.

Embracing what we have to offer the world will increase our self-esteem, which will, in turn, attract potential suitors. Confidence is sexy as hell. Another benefit to realizing our strengths is that it puts us in a better place to decide who deserves an opportunity to be in a healthy, intimate relationship with us. Instead of wasting our TME with unworthy guys, we're able to focus on quality men.

Is Your Self-Esteem Where It Needs to Be? (Quiz)

When you have made a list of your traits and done the work to truly believe them, use the checklist below to see if your self-esteem is at a point where you will have the attractive glow of confidence and make informed decisions about who is a proper match for you.

- ☐ I was able to accept at least two new positive traits about myself that I did not fully realize before.
- ☐ I'm confident that I have awareness of most of my positive traits.
- ☐ I believe the things that my friends and family members say they like about me.
- ☐ While I know I'm not perfect (no one is), I know that I have a lot more positive traits than negative.
- ☐ I understand that there are positive traits that come from growing up gay and living as a gay man.
- ☐ I feel worthy of being pursued because of all I have to offer in a relationship.
- ☐ The next time someone says something positive about me, I will not immediately discount it and will instead fairly consider whether or not it's true.

Your True Love Story: The Work Starts with the Self

Kevin (eighty-four) and Winston (eighty-three)

Together: fifty-five years

When Kevin and Winston met, they were both living in New York City. Kevin was ending his job at an organization and was turning most of his focus toward forming his own company. Starting this business meant he needed capital, and he would have events in the Hamptons in order to raise funds. Kevin and Winston met at one of the events in the spring of 1961.

At that time, Winston was acting and had realized a career in theater for a while. He was dating another actor. When he began also dating Kevin, he had to eventually decide between the two. He jokes that when he was making the decision, he had no idea it would lead to being with someone for fifty-five years.

Their first meeting was pleasant. Kevin was very attracted to Winston and had to tell himself to "go slowly" with this one. He had a history of getting caught up in superficial attractions and moving quickly in the relationship just because he thought someone was good-looking. Through seeing a therapist, Kevin was able to realize that in past relationships he moved so quickly and did not respect himself, because he saw himself as a failure. Seeing himself this way led to the relationships failing as well. Kevin realized he would have to work on his own sense of self-worth if he wanted to be able to enter into a healthy relationship. With the help of therapy, by the end of the summer, Kevin had a more realistic notion of his own value as a person, and only then did he feel comfortable enough with Winston to let things happen between them in the "fullest possible sense." Yep, that means exactly what you think it means.

Kevin was able to get to a point where he was feeling confident enough about himself and the relationship to move in together, with Winston still keeping his apartment for a while—just in case. They still reside in the apartment that they first moved into together.

References

Morrow, D. F. 2004. "Social Work Practice With Gay, Lesbian, Bisexual, and Transgender Adolescents." *Families in Society* 85 (1): 91–99.

Weber-Gilmore, G., S. Rose, and R. Rubinstein. 2011. "The Impact of Internalized Homophobia on Outness for Lesbian, Gay, and Bisexual Individuals." *The Professional Counselor* 1 (3): 163–175.

CHAPTER 3
Figure out Your True Needs

I have seen a lot of my clients enter healthy relationships once they took enough time to figure out what it was that they truly needed from a partner. Determining what you actually want from a partner may not be as easy as it seems. We may be able to easily rattle off a list of things we want from a guy, but are these things that would actually lead us into healthy relationships? Chances are, the lists we have in our heads of what we want do not match up with what would actually work for a lasting relationship. Why is that? Many external variables influence what we think we need from a partner, and they often drown out the things we actually need for ourselves. Let's go over some of the major variables.

Look Out for the Parent Trap

It's not uncommon that as gay men we fall into the "parent trap." By this I mean that we will only date guys we would want to bring home to our parents. For gay men, this could be an unhealthy issue because we may want to bring home men who we think act heterosexual enough for them to be seen as "normal" by our family.

Throughout our lives, especially in childhood, we seek our parents' acceptance, and we want to feel close to them so that we know we belong to something greater than ourselves. Being gay and feeling different from others or possibly having heard negative references to members of the LGBT community in your home may take away from feeling accepted and a part of the family. So to make up for this and gain acceptance, we will look for straight-acting men to bring home because such a partner will go along with the family norm of heterosexuality.

Are You Really Only into Masculine Guys?

A lot of gay men will only consider dating men who act extremely masculine, even outside of doing so just to please their parents. Gay men, especially when it comes to dating and sex, prefer masculine over effeminate men. Consider the large proportion of personal ads strongly stating that they possess masculine traits and are looking for men who are "straight acting" (Sanchez and Vilan 2012). This heavy emphasis on masculinity over femininity is related to negative feelings about being gay, perhaps because as boys we were teased and bullied for not meeting the masculine norm (Sanchez and Vilan 2012). It makes sense that if we are bullied for something, then we will have a negative association with it and perhaps some shame. We would want to create as much distance as possible between that "negative" and "shameful" trait and how we would like to identify. If others see feminine as bad, then that greatly increases the chances that we will also see feminine as bad.

Perhaps you are a guy who genuinely prefers a guy with more traditionally masculine traits. However, I think it's worth some soul searching to see if that is truly the case or if your preference may be based on some issues from growing up that caused you to artificially associate masculinity with a preferred way of acting. I would also recommend not necessarily eliminating all less masculine-acting men from your options to see if you may wind up finding them attractive. Realizing what your true preference is will allow you to increase your chances of picking someone who will ultimately be a good fit for you.

Do Not Go to Extremes

Another trap that people fall into is being hyper focused on looking for a particular trait from our next partners because our recent exes did not have those traits. We feel that since our previous relationships did not work, it must be because of the other people, and now to guarantee success in the next relationships, we will search out traits that the last guys did not have. For example, let's say that while you were dating a guy, you often felt that he was a bit boring for your taste, and this was something that would nag at you. Then, after you broke up, you felt that the relationship must not have worked because he was so boring, and now all you need to make the next relationship work is a fun and adventurous guy. This is a faulty theory. The truth is that there are numerous variables that would explain why a relationship did not work. Deciding on someone to date just because he possesses in spades the opposite or "missing" trait of an ex will not likely spell success. I learned this the hard way, over and over and over and over again.

What Really Matters

We also need to be careful that our general preferences do not blind us to what will actually work in a relationship. You may really like blue eyes, but do you really believe that if you meet a guy who doesn't have blue eyes, he cannot be the other half of a successful and fulfilling relationship? It's great to know what we prefer aesthetically, but establish before deciding based on a certain trait if it's a must-have attribute that will determine whether or not you could be in a fulfilling relationship with this person.

Also, try to get out of your head all of the images that the media tries to perpetuate as an ideal. Online, on television, and in movies and magazines, we get bombarded by images of what signifies beauty and what we are supposed to desire. This, too, will get in the way of us truly going after men who have what we need to be fulfilled and with whom we could be in a healthy long-term relationship. A six-pack does not in any way spell relationship success. Yes, they are pretty to look at and nice to touch, but even rock-hard abs lose their appeal and will disappear at some point—and then what?

How do we make sure we are valuing traits that truly matter to us and will therefore actually lead to healthy relationships? We need to reassess the traits we are looking for in a partner. Hopefully now you have an understanding that some of the traits you thought were so important in a guy are not actually that important to you—that you might have been valuing traits that won't contribute to the type of relationship you want. You need to look through a lens of what will make *you* happy and what would contribute to a good partner fit for *you*. Completing the Traits That Matter Work Sheet (table 1) will help you figure this out.

Do You Know Which Traits Matter? (Quiz)
Once you complete the Traits That Matter Work Sheet, you will have a more realistic understanding of the aspects you would want to see in a

potential partner. Just to be sure you have accomplished this, review the list below, and check where appropriate. You will want to have a majority of the boxes checked before moving on. If you don't, spend more time with the worksheet and this chapter.

- ☐ I'm able to summarize at least three things I need from a partner in an intimate relationship.
- ☐ I'm able to distinguish between what I want from a partner versus what will please my parents.
- ☐ I'm able to distinguish between what I want from a partner versus what I may be avoiding due to internalized homophobia.
- ☐ I'm able to distinguish between what I want from a partner versus what the media tells me I should want.
- ☐ I was surprised by at least two items that wound up not being as important to me as I thought they might be.
- ☐ I was surprised by at least two items that wound up being more important than I would have initially thought.

Your True Love Story: What Matters Most
Jim (sixty-three) and Puck (sixty-eight)

Together: forty-three years

When Jim and Puck first met, Jim had just returned from a year in Europe teaching. He was living in San Francisco with his best friend and was trying to figure out what to do with his life. He had pursued a number of paths for a living and now wanted to decide what to focus on. Outside of the career issue, Jim was having a great time being a gay man in the City by the Bay.

Puck was not faring as well as Jim at the time. He felt like he was at low point in his life. Puck had just completed directing two shows, but he was excluded from both the credits and the profits earned. He was feeling "royally screwed" and "disillusioned." He was also in a confused place personally, as he was living a gay life but also dating women.

Jim and Puck had met several times before they started dating. They were both members of a small community of spiritual seekers in San Francisco. During a year or two of them both being a part of this community, neither registered attraction for the other. Puck believes that Jim was not into him because he had a very distinctive way of dressing. Puck was a dancer, so he wore tight clothes with flowing scarves. Jim does admit that at the time he thought Puck was "a wild dresser."

One evening, they were at a bar on Polk Street, each dancing separately. They began talking and then dancing with each other. Puck felt attracted to Jim then and thought that he was leaving with him; however, Jim thought Puck was leaving with Jim's best friend—not realizing that Puck was attracted to him. They went back to Jim's place. While listening to music, the friend announced that he was going to bed, and Jim thought about how he was being "left alone with this guy I didn't much like." To Jim's surprise, they wound up having good energy and great conversations about politics, Joni Mitchell, viewpoints, music, and even scarves. They felt as if they were very similar and quite complementary. The experience of that night was enough to make them realize that they saw something special in the other.

Jim realized that his initial dislike of Puck was based on superficial traits that were not actually critical in figuring out whether or not Puck could be a match for him. He admits that had he not looked past the surface, they never would have had a chance to talk and discover how much of a fit they were. Because Jim was able to pay attention to what truly matters in making a match, for over forty years they have enjoyed a relationship where they support each other completely.

Reference
Sanchez, F. J., and E. Vilan. 2012. "Straight-Acting Gays: The Relationship Between Masculine Consciousness, Anti-Effeminacy, and Negative Gay Identity." *Archives of Sexual Behavior* 41: 111–119.

Traits That Matter (Work Sheet)
Rate on a scale of one to ten (one being low and ten being high) the importance that each of these traits has for you in order to be in a healthy relationship.

When using this tool, be mindful of what makes *you* happy and what *you* want from a partner instead of the images you may have in your head of what the media or society says you should want. Try not to worry about how these traits are viewed by others, including friends and family members.

Traits are in no particular order, and there are spaces for you to add any others to the list.

Masculine	1 2 3 4 5 6 7 8 9 10
Feminine	1 2 3 4 5 6 7 8 9 10
Smart	1 2 3 4 5 6 7 8 9 10

Hipster	1 2 3 4 5 6 7 8 9 10
Geeky	1 2 3 4 5 6 7 8 9 10
Twinky	1 2 3 4 5 6 7 8 9 10
Muscular	1 2 3 4 5 6 7 8 9 10
Cub	1 2 3 4 5 6 7 8 9 10
Bear	1 2 3 4 5 6 7 8 9 10
Otter	1 2 3 4 5 6 7 8 9 10
Younger	1 2 3 4 5 6 7 8 9 10
Older	1 2 3 4 5 6 7 8 9 10
Kind	1 2 3 4 5 6 7 8 9 10
Generous	1 2 3 4 5 6 7 8 9 10
Affectionate	1 2 3 4 5 6 7 8 9 10
Enjoys similar activities	1 2 3 4 5 6 7 8 9 10
Good sense of humor	1 2 3 4 5 6 7 8 9 10
HIV-	1 2 3 4 5 6 7 8 9 10
HIV+	1 2 3 4 5 6 7 8 9 10
Wants children	1 2 3 4 5 6 7 8 9 10
Wants monogamy	1 2 3 4 5 6 7 8 9 10
Wants an open relationship	1 2 3 4 5 6 7 8 9 10
Large genitals	1 2 3 4 5 6 7 8 9 10
Tops	1 2 3 4 5 6 7 8 9 10
Bottoms	1 2 3 4 5 6 7 8 9 10
Is versatile	1 2 3 4 5 6 7 8 9 10
Good communicator	1 2 3 4 5 6 7 8 9 10
Adventurous	1 2 3 4 5 6 7 8 9 10
Stylish	1 2 3 4 5 6 7 8 9 10
Tall	1 2 3 4 5 6 7 8 9 10
Short	1 2 3 4 5 6 7 8 9 10
Honest	1 2 3 4 5 6 7 8 9 10
Popular	1 2 3 4 5 6 7 8 9 10

Reliable	1 2 3 4 5 6 7 8 9 10
Shares emotions	1 2 3 4 5 6 7 8 9 10
Creative	1 2 3 4 5 6 7 8 9 10
Financially stable	1 2 3 4 5 6 7 8 9 10
Wealthy	1 2 3 4 5 6 7 8 9 10
Ethnicity/race: _____	1 2 3 4 5 6 7 8 9 10
Eye color: _____	1 2 3 4 5 6 7 8 9 10
Skin tone: _____	1 2 3 4 5 6 7 8 9 10
Hair color: _____	1 2 3 4 5 6 7 8 9 10
_____	1 2 3 4 5 6 7 8 9 10
_____	1 2 3 4 5 6 7 8 9 10
_____	1 2 3 4 5 6 7 8 9 10
_____	1 2 3 4 5 6 7 8 9 10
_____	1 2 3 4 5 6 7 8 9 10

General guide on how to interpret your ratings:

1–5 = Take it or leave it.

5–7 = It would be nice but not a must.

7–10 = I deserve to be happy, and a partner with this trait will make me happy.

CHAPTER 4
Make Use of Past Relationships

Often, when thinking of past relationships, a lot of us tend to think that all they are good for are heartbreak, sadness, and drama—baggage that you worry about bringing into your new relationship. This need not be the case. There is a lot of learning you can take from a past relationship in order to make your next relationship that much stronger. I will show you how to turn that baggage into assets.

Every Relationship Deserves Some Grieving

All past relationships deserved to be grieved, even if the relationship was toxic and one that you should not have been in. You would not necessarily be grieving the guy or the actual relationship but instead likely grieving what you wanted out of the relationship that you did not get. It's important to pay attention to and respect what you wished for that did not come to fruition. So even if the relationship was bad, take time to think about what it was you wanted and how you feel about not getting that. My guess would be that you feel sad and angry and perhaps experience some shame or guilt about not having ended the relationship sooner (or getting into it in the first place). Allow yourself to feel those emotions so that you are able to get some relief around sadness and anger. Eventually, you can freely move on to another relationship. Also, try to be realistic, and have some self-compassion about the shame or guilt you may be feeling. When starting the relationship, you likely did not have the skills necessary to enter into a healthy one, so you thought you were doing the right thing.

The opposite of the toxic relationship would be one that you experienced as fantastic and in which you thought the guy was great. With these types of relationships, grieving tends to be around the loss of the person in addition to the relationship itself. With this type of loss, you also want to be sure to pay attention to the feelings coming up for you, which may be more types of emotions than what you might experience from a toxic relationship. Feelings may include anger, sadness, shame or guilt, fear (that you will not find another relationship that works so well), and happiness or love (when you think of certain memories). Again, you want to give yourself the time and freedom to experience these emotions.

How to Give Your Feelings the Attention They Deserve

All feelings are supposed to be temporary; they are meant to come and go. This is the case if you acknowledge and experience your feelings. However, if you do not give your feelings the attention they deserve, then they will never leave and will creep up at inconvenient times, causing you to feel extra stressed, sad, or scared and possibly causing you to act in irrational ways. Ever take your anger out on someone who was not the source of it or overreact to a situation? Those are examples of your past emotions letting you know that they want to be dealt with.

How do you deal with your feelings when it comes to relationships? Try this. Recall a strong memory from the relationship, and then tune into your body and notice what is happening. Are you feeling tightness in your chest? Are you experiencing heaviness on your shoulders? Is there a cramping in your stomach? Whatever you feel, stay with it, and lean into it, however uncomfortable. After spending some time with the feeling in your body, attempt to label the emotion causing the physical sensation. Giving it a name should offer some relief. Then "ask" that emotion what it needs for some relief (Frederick 2009). That feeling may make "suggestions," such as needing an apology, for you to get rid of the ex-boyfriend's stuff you have in your closet, or for you to radically accept the loss of the relationship.

When You Are Done, Make Sure You Are Done

Ending relationships is difficult, especially ones that were long-term. Not only do we become emotionally attached and used to being with those people, but our bodies also have become used to being with and around them, making detaching from them seem even more like an impossibility. However, it's not impossible and needs to happen if you want to enter a healthy relationship with someone else. The first step to detaching is realizing how attached you are. If you are honest with yourself about how emotionally and physically connected you were to that person, then you could realistically give yourself the necessary time, distance, and support to get over him.

I'm sure you have heard this a hundred times, but here goes a hundred and one to make sure you get it: nothing substitutes for time when it comes to a breakup. Your body and mind need the actual time to forget the impression this person had on you. Time will also allow you to see your situation in a more realistic perspective, instead of mostly idealizing the relationship and thinking that everything about it or him was perfect when, in reality, it was not. Do not linger. When the relationship ends, even if you want to be friends, give yourself distance for a while so that you are able to heal from and grieve for the romantic part of the relationship. Still talking with each other and seeing each other will not allow the mind and body what they need to understand that you are no longer in a romantic relationship. Also, time still spent with him is time in your already-busy life that you could likely spend actually doing the work to get over him and get yourself in a place where you are ready to enter another relationship. The relationship very likely ended for good reasons; sticking around each other makes it so much more likely that you will get sucked back into a relationship that did not work the first time around, wasting your TME.

Giving yourself this necessary time and space could likely prove difficult. Get some help. Regardless of whether your friends were behind the relationship or not, you will need them to be supportive of you while you grieve and get over the relationship. Throughout the book, I will speak to the importance of making use of your friends. They are vital to many aspects of your getting into a healthy relationship. Here they will serve you by listening to how you are feeling about the breakup, providing occasional distraction, reminding you of how precious you are, and supporting your decision to end the relationship or to stay away from it. Some of my clients will not go to their friends, especially if their friends did not like the guy, because they do not want to seem to be a burden, or they feel shame, or they are worried about hearing, "I told you so." If their friends really liked the guy, they are concerned about seeming like a failure. Your friends are your friends for a reason. Trust that they will give you what you need if you reach out to them. I would imagine that if your friends needed this type of attention from you, you would provide it to them. Allow them to do the same.

Learn from Experience

Once you have grieved the relationship and are secure in not falling back into it, then it's time to do yourself a great service and take a look at what occurred during your relationship for information that may help you in your next one. Good or bad, what you spent your time building with someone else is a great learning experience. First, since hindsight is 20/20, you'll want to see if now you are able to recognize any red flags that were present when you first started to get to know the guy. Was he late to your initial dates? Did he seem to talk about his ex-boyfriend a bit too much? Did he seem distracted when you were letting him know intimate details of your life? For each person, the red flags will vary, so just think back, and try to see what sticks out to you as something that you did not like but decided to overlook. There will always be aspects of the other person that you do not like, but you need to discern how important those aspects are to you when it comes to a long-term relationship. Your Traits That Matter Work Sheet is extremely helpful with figuring this out.

You also want to pay attention to relationship patterns that you may fall into that are not healthy for you. Most of us grow up with the model of our parents for how relationships should look. If our parents had unhealthy relationships, then we may tend to naturally recreate those types of relationships because that is all we know. We did not have a class in school that taught us the skills necessary to build and maintain healthy relationships. As gay men, we are at an even further loss because we likely did not see many same-sex relationships from which we could learn. So we are fending for ourselves and learning by trial and error. Examine your past relationships to see if you fall into a pattern similar to your parents'. Figure out if this is what you want or if these patterns fit your needs. If not, be aware of the behavior and situations you would want to avoid in the future when starting a new relationship. Even though your parents were your model, that does not mean you cannot learn new skills in order to get your individual needs met in a healthy manner. You are able to pick up new skills through learning from current relationships around you that you admire or by seeing a therapist.

Along with being aware of patterns you may fall into, you'll want to be aware overall of what worked and did not work for you in regards to the relationship. Think back on your ex and the relationship, and recall what made you smile or laugh, what warmed your heart, and what stimulated you. Also, you want to consider what made you feel sad, angry, or shameful. You will want to replicate the positive aspects and situations that you recall in a new relationship by considering men who have these aspects to them or by recreating the types of situations (be they activities or behaviors like lots of hugging, if that's something you enjoyed) in your next relationship. When you know what your needs are, then you have the power to be direct in your actions to make sure you get them met.

A Relationship Ending Does Not Equal Failure

Often people will equate a relationship ending with the relationship failing. This is not necessarily the case. Just because a relationship came to an end does not mean that it failed. Most romantic relationships in a person's lifetime do not last forever. As I mentioned, we did not have a class where we learned the skills to be in a relationship. So we have to learn along the way, which means that we are not very likely to know enough about ourselves and our needs by the time we have our first relationships to have those be healthy ones that will last a long time. It is extremely rare to hit a home run your first time at bat. (Surprise! I bet you were not expecting a sports comparison in this book.) We learn about ourselves partly through going through romantic relationships and having them end. We learn about how we tend to behave when we spend a lot of time around other people in an intimate manner. We get an understanding of what we need from our partners and what we are able to authentically give as partners. If we are smart, when we learn these things, we pay attention to them and make use of the information to change our behaviors and choices in our next relationships. Doing so will increase the chances that the next relationship is forever. An experience that helped you get to know yourself and your needs better (and likely consisted of some good times) should not be seen as a failure because it ended.

Are You Ready to Move On? (Quiz)

Getting over a breakup and feeling good about past relationships are not easy accomplishments. Hopefully the words in this chapter have helped you to be able to do both. To be sure that you are over your ex and that you have made use of your past relationships as learning experiences, fill out the checklist below. If you are able to check all the boxes, then you are ready and better prepared to enter your next relationship.

- ☐ I have paid attention to and given some quality time to the emotions brought up for me when I think about past relationships.
- ☐ I have turned to at least one friend to share my feelings and experience of a past breakup.
- ☐ I honestly feel that I have given myself enough time to grieve.
- ☐ I honestly feel that I have given myself enough distance from my ex in order to not foolishly fall back into our relationship.
- ☐ I'm able to list at least three things I learned from past relationships about myself and how to better behave in a relationship to get my needs met.
- ☐ I appreciate the learning from any and all relationships.

Your True Love Story: Dealing with the Past before Moving On to the Future
Adam (forty-five) and Tony (fifty-seven)

Together: eighteen years

Prior to meeting Tony, Adam had been in a dysfunctional relationship for two years. This relationship was a toxic one for Adam mostly because before entering the relationship, he had not yet learned self-respect. He entered the relationship at age twenty-three by having a one-night stand with someone and deciding to make a long-term relationship out of it, even though there was no real reason to think that this person was a match for him. Adam admits, "I clung on to it like a cat hanging from a tree with my claws." Throughout the relationship, though they agreed to be monogamous, the guy cheated on him, transmitting STIs to Adam. This was not enough to make Adam leave—again, because of the lack of self-respect. Even after being hit by his boyfriend, Adam decided to stay in the relationship. It was difficult for him to leave because he felt unloved by others and thought this boyfriend was giving him the love that he needed.

Throughout the relationship, Adam became more aware that he lacked self-compassion and self-worth. This awareness allowed him to begin to gain enough self-esteem so that when the boyfriend let him know that he was going to visit a friend in Florida and was taking someone else with him instead of Adam, Adam decided to end the relationship. Ever since then, he has been an independent and strong person and has never looked to get back into that relationship. Adam learned from that relationship what he would and would not accept from a partner.

After that relationship, he was single for two years, carefree, and not feeling a strong need to enter a relationship. He was dating, however, and went to a to New Year's Eve party with a date who wound up drinking a lot that night. The date drank enough that he had to head up to the room where they were staying so that he could sleep. Adam stayed at the party, and along came Tony.

Adam and Tony dated for two months before deciding to be exclusive and make their relationship official. Adam, having learned from his past relationship the importance of paying attention to his needs, waited two years before moving in with Tony, to help make sure it was the right decision for them. They believed that certain aspects of their relationship should not be rushed in order to avoid irrational decisions. Adam wanted to make sure that they trusted each other enough before taking such a big step.

They have now been together for eighteen years, thanks in part to Adam using the lessons learned from his previous relationship to help him better enter something extremely special with Tony.

Reference

Frederick, R. J. 2009. *Living Like You Mean It: Use the Wisdom and Power of Your Emotions to Get the Life You Really Want.* San Francisco, CA: Jossey-Bass.

CHAPTER 5
Decide How to Meet

So this is the part you were waiting for: how to actually go out and get that guy.

Once you have gotten rid of the disadvantage of being desperate, have really figured out what you have to offer others, thoroughly assessed what is actually important to you in a relationship, and made sure to be over past relationships, you will be able to make the most out of this next part of the book. Now is when we get strategic about how you look for your match. Again, you want to be strategic so that you increase your chances of finding someone worthy of being in a relationship with you and do not waste your TME on the quest to find him.

As I mentioned earlier, you most likely did not learn in school or from your parents how to pick up quality guys. You did not likely receive instruction on where to meet guys who would be a good fit for you. Nor was there likely advice on how best to manage your first date to get what you want from it and then know once you start a relationship whether or not it's a good one for you. Well, now you get that instruction. This section will help you avoid typical traps that we fall into when looking for a partner. It will help you figure out the places specific to you that make the most sense to find your match. Then fast-forward a few months; I will help you assess whether or not you have gotten yourself into a healthy relationship.

The Truth about the Bar Scene

For many of us gay men, when we think about getting out there to meet someone, we tend to think about bars. They are great places to socialize with new people; however, I'm not aware of any great number of healthy relationships that started out at a bar. This is for a few reasons.

(1) We all know that while alcohol may lower our inhibitions and allow us to be more social, it also lowers our standards of who we find attractive physically or appealing in terms of personality. With the assistance of this book, you have done the work to know that you are worthy of a great match. Why would you handicap your chances of finding that quality guy by making decisions if you are not in your most sound mind? I'm not saying that if you like to drink, you shouldn't drink at bars. I *am* saying that you should be aware of what alcohol will do to your ability to make accurate decisions about who is a good match for you. If you enjoy drinking alcohol, drink and enjoy yourself and your friends; just know that in a bar, especially with "martini goggles," finding Mr. Right is not likely.

(2) Alcohol not only lowers our standards about who we find attractive physically or appealing in terms of personality, but it also lowers our standards of whether we are looking to establish a quality match or want to just go home with someone. Just going home with someone could be fun, but, more often than not, doing so decreases your overall chance of entering into

a healthy relationship because instead of perhaps something that makes sense long term, what will likely happen is either a one-night stand or something you try to turn into a relationship that will not work because it started with just wanting sex. Again, one-night stands could be fun, but if you continue to place most of your dating energy into going to bars and having them, you will be taking a lot of TME away from opportunities that are so much more likely to get you into a healthy relationship.

(3) Even if you're at a bar and not drinking, the chances of meeting a good match are low because there are so many different types of guys around us at a bar. They will have such varied interests, personalities, priorities, and lifestyles that they are not likely to be a match. All we can say that we *may* have in common with these guys is that they like the same bar and that they are gay. But even this is not a given as they could have been dragged to the bar by friends, or they are heterosexual. Even if all the men were gay, do not demean yourself by thinking a guy is a match for you just because he's gay. I know I hated it when people would think that I would be "perfect" for their friend because he was also gay. Do yourself a favor, and do not inflict this same nonsense on yourself.

I understand that bars are one of the few places where we are able to be pretty sure that everyone around us is gay or bisexual. And, again, I understand that bars can be fun for socializing and enjoying ourselves, and I know that there are couples in healthy relationships who did meet at a bar. However, we would increase our chances of meeting a match for us by not spending so much of our partner-finding energy on bar experiences.

Hook-Up Apps Are for Hooking Up

Similar to bar experiences, hook-up apps will likely lead you to sex but not to a healthy long-term relationship. No matter what a guy writes in his profile on these apps, chances are that he is likely looking for sex. Even if two people are looking to date long-term and are on these apps, the connotation behind these apps is hooking up, so a connection is likely to lead to sex. Using these apps could be fun, but they are very unlikely to lead you into a healthy relationship. With the limited amount of information on the apps, chances are that you would not be able to determine if you have enough variables in common with someone else on the app to lead to something substantial in terms of a partner match.

Online Dating Sites Are Worth a Try

An online option that will serve you better than apps in terms of finding a healthy partner fit is online dating sites. While they also could be used for hooking up, they do still have some connotation of meeting a love match. In order to increase the chances that you find a match on these sites that will turn into a healthy relationship, I recommend the following.

(1) Once you have exchanged a few chats or e-mails with someone and he interests you enough to want to keep communicating, then just meet (at a place where you feel safe meeting) sooner rather than later. Before we go on first dates, we often have fantasies in our heads of what these new guys will be like. Our lack of actual knowledge of what these people are actually like will allow us to fill in these unknowns with our own fantasies of what we want them to be like. The longer we correspond with people before meeting them, the more we build up our

fantasies and become invested in ideas of what to expect from them. The longer we wait to meet them, the less likely it is that they will live up to our fantasies—and the more likely we are to be disappointed and not give ourselves a fair chance to see if they may actually be a good fit for us.

(2) Make the most efficient use of your profile. This means incorporating the positive attributes you learned about yourself and what you're looking for in a guy into your profile. Pictures are obviously key to be initially looked at. In addition to physically flattering pictures, make sure that yours reflect your personality, your interests, and your best smile. Most other users are likely only going to put their most physically flattering pictures up, so any potential match will be seeing a lot of these kinds of shots. If you post a picture of you doing something that you love to do and someone else is also into that activity, then you're more likely to be grabbing the attention of someone who has something important in common with you. Also, when doing something you enjoy, you're more likely to be radiating positivity, which is sexy.

(3) Keep your profile honest. If you do not plan on ever meeting the guy, then, sure, there is plenty you're able to get away with if you're not honest. However, our work here is to enter healthy relationships. You will not be able to initiate a healthy relationship when lying plays a role from the beginning. Also, you're going to meet and hopefully spend time together. Your lies will become obvious, and you will have wound up just wasting your TME and his. Lying could wind up hurting you beyond just the guys you're dating. The gay community could prove to be a small world even in big urban areas with large gay populations. You do not want a reputation as a liar to precede you, making it more difficult for you to meet quality guys.

(4) When looking at others' profiles, make sure you have your Traits That Matter Work Sheet with you so that you're able to easily remind yourself of what really will contribute to a healthy relationship for you. This will avoid your getting caught up in someone's amazing abs or dimples and thinking he must be your match.

That's What Friends Are For

So now let's migrate from the digital world of meeting your match to real-world options. My most recommended method for meeting your match is increasing your network of people who care about you and want to see you happy—in other words, friends. This is your most efficient use of TME. Friends tend to have similar traits to us and tend to have our best interests at heart, so if they know we want to be in relationships, they will likely do some work in keeping an eye out for people they think would be compatible. As I mentioned earlier, as gay men, we often have had to deal with (heterosexual) friends thinking we are "just perfect" for friends of theirs just because they are also gay. So to avoid this, have a talk with your friends about the kind of guys you're into. If you're comfortable doing so, you could even share your completed Traits That Matter Work Sheet with them so they really have an understanding of what you're looking for and how serious you are about entering a healthy relationship. Making use of our friends makes sense because it's putting qualified eyes and ears out there to bring possible matches our way.

Do What You Like

I also highly recommend becoming involved on a regular basis in activities that you enjoy. Whether that is rock climbing, pottery, a certain genre of books, movies, theater, music, or a particular cause you would like to volunteer for, find something you like. Doing things we enjoy allows us to be in the presence of people who enjoy the same things as us, which increases our chances of making real connections either with potential boyfriends or friends—and the friend connection could lead us to boyfriends. Also, when we are doing something that we enjoy, our moods tend to be positive, and this positivity radiating from us is extremely attractive to others. So when engaging in an activity we enjoy, we get to feel good and put ourselves in a space to meet people with similar traits. Depending on where we live, we may be able to ask around or do an online search to figure out if there is a gay-male or LGBT group that meets around what we are interested in. A well-known option for finding groups is meetup.com. While the site is not LGBT specific, you're able to search for LGBT-specific groups. You may also want to check with LGBT community centers that may be nearby to see if they have group activities centered on a specific topic.

When figuring out what your interest are, be careful not to pick things that you think you're supposed to be into, such as the latest exercise trend. Take some time to think about what you look forward to doing, what you could see yourself doing for hours, or what puts a smile on your face when you think of doing it.

Still need help figuring out what your interests are? Or maybe you need help finding an interest that includes others? To get some help with this and to increase the likelihood that you will actually partake in those activities, complete the Interests Work Sheet (table 2).

The great thing about my top choices for how to find your relationship match is that not only do they greatly increase your likelihood of meeting a quality partner, they also contribute to a fulfilling life in general. Making friends and engaging in activities we enjoy make our lives that much more worth experiencing.

How to Approach Your Prospects

So you're doing an activity you enjoy and see an attractive guy, and it seems like he's enjoying himself. Do you wait around in hopes that he will come up to you? Not at all. Be assertive. By not just waiting for the guy to approach you, you're increasing the chances of meeting him and therefore the opportunities to meet your love match. Also, the confidence it showcases will likely be deemed appealing by the guy you're after—whether or not he was initially into you.

If he is with a group of friends, you should not just intrude on their conversation. You will want to get closer to the group, try to subtly get his attention, and let him know you're interested. A smile and a nod may be all you need. Once you have his attention, your goal is to have an opportunity for just the two of you to be together to speak. Again, a slight tilt of the head may be all you need to get him to excuse himself from his friends and come over. If he is alone, feel free to approach, walking over with a genuine smile and as much confidence as you can muster. To help with that confidence, remind yourself of all the great qualities you have to offer.

Once you're together, try to be genuine in your approach, so stand the way you would normally stand, and speak like you normally would; this means no cheesy pick-up lines. You will want to start by introducing yourself and giving him the opportunity to do the same. Once the introductions are over, if you like something about him (what he is wearing, his eyes, or his hair), tell him in a way that shows some vulnerability. So instead of saying, "That's a cool jacket," or "Your eyes are hot," let him know that *you* like those traits: "Your jacket caught my eye. I think it looks really nice on you," or, "I was really taken by your eyes. I think they're quite attractive." This will be more flattering than making generic comments about him and will allow him to connect with you a bit more because you're being vulnerable. If he's not interested, he'll let you know (in one way or another), and you then can let him know that it was nice meeting him and make your way back to where you were. Upon returning to where you were, you should pat yourself on the back (though not literally) for being courageous and going for what you wanted. Obviously your match will be into you and available, so when that is not the case, do not waste your TME, and move on.

If the introduction does go well and he wants to continue talking, keep the conversation light and the amount of time you wind up speaking short. Stay away from heavy or invasive topics. During this initial meeting, you want to get to know just enough about him to figure out whether or not he is first-date material. You also want to make sure he knows enough about you in order to make the same determination. Some safe conversation topics would include whether he is having a good time wherever you are, what he normally does to enjoy himself, positive or humorous (but in good taste) comments about what is happening where you are, and more about the activity that you're engaged in (be it rock climbing or a networking event). Also, you want your first date to be special and more involved than this impromptu meeting, especially if he is with friends. I would recommend not spending more than twenty minutes on this initial meeting. After the twenty minutes, let him down easy if you're no longer interested ("I'm going to head out now. I hope you enjoy the rest of your night"), or, if you are, ask if he would be interested in exchanging contact information, letting him know that you're interested in getting together ("I really enjoyed speaking with you. Would you be interested in getting together sometime?"). If he's not interested in getting together, you should head back to where you were, and on the way, pat yourself on the back for your efforts. If he does want to exchange contact information, then great; you may have a first date in your future.

I use the word "may" when referring to that first date because there is still some work to be done to make sure the date happens. If you really did feel as if you were interested in the guy, then do not play waiting games. Just contact him when you would like and set up a plan for your date. As with the initial meeting, you want to keep the time figuring out the first date short and light. Save the big talks for your first date, not for over the phone, where conversations could be misunderstood since you're not seeing the person's face and can't read his body language. To help keep it light, you should have some ideas of where to go before contacting him (I offer tips on picking the perfect place for your first date in the next chapter). Also, as I suggested with online dating, try to meet as soon as possible. The longer you wait to meet, the more of a fantasy of what you want this guy to be will build up (versus who he really is), and you will tend to be more disappointed when you finally meet him.

If he does not return your call or is supposed to contact you and does not, pat yourself on the back again for your work at getting this far, and know that by continuing to do this work, you're increasing your chances of getting to that first date with a guy who will be your match.

Do You Know How to Best Meet the Man of Your Dreams? (Quiz)

While you could meet the love of your life anywhere, taking the above guidance will increase the likelihood that you are putting your TME into something that is more likely to turn into a healthy relationship. Fill out the checklist below. If you have most of the boxes checked, then (hooray!) you have the needed understanding of how to best meet a potential boyfriend.

- ☐ I agree that the men at gay bars are so varied in terms of personality that finding a match at one would be difficult.
- ☐ I understand that the mood and atmosphere of a bar may lead to fun times and encounters; however, these do not tend to translate into a foundation for a healthy relationship.
- ☐ I get that guy-finding apps are basically for hooking up.
- ☐ There are changes I could make to my online dating profile to be more efficient in finding a relationship match (if applicable).
- ☐ I see the value in partaking in activities I enjoy and letting my friends know the kind of guys I'm into in order to increase the likelihood of meeting someone with whom I have things in common.

Your True Love Story: Online Leading to In Love

Sam (thirty-three) and David (thirty-five)

Together: seven years

When Sam and David met, Sam was twenty-six years old and had just gotten out of a three-and-a-half-year relationship four months prior. He was living on his own for the first time ever. Before that, he had lived with roommates and then with his boyfriend. For Sam, this was a transitional period, with him being uncertain of his future. He was wrapping up graduate school and feeling restless, unsettled, and overall not sure what his next step would be.

At this same time, David was twenty-eight and three years prior had moved to the city where Sam was living without knowing anyone there. He was just getting his feet on the ground in terms of his career.

Sam was going to the gay bars after his breakup, mostly because his friends were going to bars. However, he was not counting only on bars to meet quality guys; Sam realized that going online might be a great way to meet someone who would be a good match for him.

Sam and David met in a chat room, wrote to each other for a bit that night, and then continued to communicate throughout that week. Each felt that when speaking to people online, you're able to get a sense if there is some sort of connection there and whether or not the other person is looking for a potential relationship or just sex. They chose not to trade pictures until they were ready to meet, as they each felt the physical aspect of what was going on between them was secondary to the emotional attachment they were making. They enjoyed their chats and connection, so they decided that they should just meet.

By midweek, they had made plans to meet up for dinner that weekend. They each wanted to keep it casual, so they planned to meet at a local pizza place. During the date, they talked for hours. After the date, they traded a couple of text messages and did not speak that following week.

Sam then decided to call David that weekend to make plans as he liked where things were going between them. However, David did not respond. This had Sam question his thinking, and he was now feeling, *Well, that's not working.* The truth was that it was working, but David was practically sleeping all day for three days because he was sick; he was not responding to anyone. When David finally did respond, Sam was relieved. They talked for a while and decided to meet the following weekend for dinner. During this date, again they talked for hours, this time meeting at 7:00 p.m. for dinner and staying out until 1:00 a.m. Sam left the date knowing he wanted to kiss David.

For their next date, Sam invited David over to watch a movie. "That was kind of it" for Sam; he knew he had met someone he would want to continue dating. During this date, they kissed. A few weeks later, around Valentine's Day, they discussed how neither was dating anyone else and decided to make it more official that they were exclusive.

Seven years later, they are in a supportive and loving relationship and extremely grateful they each landed in that chat room that first night.

Interests (Work Sheet)

To properly fill out this sheet, spend time brainstorming (perhaps with a friend) activities or causes that capture your interest. They could make you feel happy, excited, or motivated. Make sure to also consider past passions that may make sense for you to revisit.

Interests   How to Partake

1.

2.

3.

4.

5.

6.

CHAPTER 6
Have the Best First Date

After all of your hard work, you're now ready for your first date. It's perfectly normal to be nervous about how you will come across on a first date and how things will play out during the date. To help with those nerves, I recommend that you try to remind yourself that a date is a time for you to enjoy yourself. Yes, you're looking for your romantic match, but please know that enjoying yourself on the date will help you with this. As I mentioned, when doing activities that you love, you radiate positivity, and this is attractive to others. Actually enjoying yourself on a date will have the same effect. So how do you make sure to enjoy your date? Let's figure that out now.

Picking the Perfect Place

When trying to figure out a place to have your date, your Interests Work Sheet will prove quite valuable. From those activities, you will want to pick something that does the following:

- Takes place in a public space
- Will last at least thirty minutes and has an option to be over in an hour or an hour and a half

- You know the other person likes to do
- Has a noise level that allows for easy conversation
- Is a comfortable space for two men to meet on a date
- Is easy for each of you to get to

And if you pick something that is outdoors, do have a backup indoor plan that also meets as many of these criteria as possible in case the weather gets in the way of outdoor plans.

I want to explain a bit about some of the points above before we move on. Picking a place from your Interests Work Sheet should help you have a good time on the date because you're doing something that you enjoy. While enjoying yourself, you also want to make sure to be safe, so a public space around others should allow for this. I find that you will want to give the date at least thirty minutes in order for each of you to settle your nerves a bit. Becoming a bit calmer will allow you to both present yourselves in a more accurate light.

While you want to then have some time to get to know each other, you do not want the date to lack a predetermined time that it could end. This is mostly helpful if the date is not going well. With a set end time, you have a reasonable explanation for finishing the date. So if the activity lasts an hour or an hour and a half, that should give you enough time to have gotten to know if this is someone that you consider a match. If he does not seem like a match and you're not enjoying yourself, then you have the activity coming to an end as a reason to end the date as well. This will help prevent you from having to make up excuses to leave, which could make a bad impression. While this guy may not be your match right now, he may be in the future, or he may wind up being friends with your match, and you do not want to have a bad reputation when it comes to dating. If the date is going well, then you could always offer to extend your time with that activity or move on to something else. This means not having something scheduled right after the date is supposed to end. Having to leave if you would prefer to stay will not only unnecessarily kill the mood and the potential for an epic first date, but it will also show that you did not think enough about the date to consider that it might go well. It could come across as insulting and does not do justice to all the hard work you have put into the process up until this point.

It's Not You; It's Him

Before we discuss how to end the date, I need to make sure that you're aware of a very important concept that is particularly helpful when dating. When people make decisions, they are making them because of what is going on for them and not because of you. Issues related to things like childhood, how they were brought up, how they feel about their choices in life, how they feel about themselves, or how their day at work went will determine people's moods, behavior, and choices. We really do not have as great of an influence on how others behave as we think we do. So if a guy decides that he does not want a second date with you, this does not mean that something is wrong with you or that you have failed at something. It just means that for various reasons, most having to do with him, he is not interested in going on another date. Possible explanations could be that he realized that he was not ready for dating, he is still stuck on an ex, you triggered something for him that he personally has an aversion to or causes him discomfort, he is prioritizing other things in his life, or he is just not into you. Even his not being into you is not about something being wrong with you; it's about his preferences based on how he grew up and what he has experienced.

Because most of us do take things personally and have for most of our lives, this concept may take time to really understand and believe. To help you realize this concept as true, I recommend thinking about it in terms of yourself. Think about how often you do things because of your own stuff going on and not because of someone else. For example, I get nervous during large social events and therefore turn inward. This may be perceived by others as me ignoring them because of something they did or me just not liking them, when in actuality it's just about my own coping skill being activated to help me in this type of situation.

So when you start to be hard on yourself because you believe you failed in some way because a guy was not interested, remind yourself that people make decisions based on what is happening for them, not based on something "wrong" with you. If you're able to accomplish this, your thinking will be based in reality, and you will avoid a lot of unnecessary pain and heartache.

This concept is especially important to remember if he does not show up for the first date. The idea sounds awful, but it does happen. Besides being disrespectful and inconsiderate, just not showing on a first date is an obvious sign that this person is not a match for you and made the decision to not show based on his own issues that don't have anything to do with you.

How to Wrap Things Up

OK, now we can move on to the end of the date. If you feel as if you would like a second date because he seems like a good match and you would like to spend more time with him, then make sure when you end the date that you show some interest in meeting again. You could do so verbally by letting him know that you enjoyed your time together. It may be difficult to be vulnerable and risk having him not say the same thing in return, but it's worth the risk so that you get a chance to show your confidence and to make sure he knows you're interested. And if you're able to remember and truly understand that if he does not want a second date, it's about him, not you, then taking the risk will not be so difficult. There is no need to figure out the details of the next date when ending this date; you could always follow up with that later. If the two of you will be figuring out the details later, then I advise that you be the one to initiate the contact. This will help alleviate any stress of waiting for him to contact you and will allow you to figure out the next date when you're ready to do so. However, if, by chance, you both read this book, then you will both have to fight it out to see who will contact whom first—good luck!

If you're not interested in a second date because it's obvious that this guy is not a match and you do not want to spend more time with him, then also be honest about this. You do not have to let him know at the end of the date that you aren't interested, but don't say that you are if you're not, and do not say you're going to contact him if that is not your intention. Remember, even if you're not interested, you do not want to burn any bridges. Whether you let him know at the end of the date or later that you're not interested in a second date, a gracious way to go about this is to let him know that you're glad you were able to meet, mention one thing about the date that you enjoyed, and then let him know that you're not looking to have a second date.

Sex on the First Date?

Let's tackle one important question for many regarding the end of a first date: to have sex or not to have sex? On this date you have two guys. The testosterone is going. You're hitting it off. You want to know if he tops or bottoms. These are all good reasons to want to have sex with someone. So if that is what you both want, then go for it. However, go for it knowing that there is a possibility that having sex so soon into the courting process could adversely affect your chances of beginning a relationship with this person. Let me explain why it might.

If sex the first time is not mind blowing, this could fill you with doubt as to whether this person is truly a match for you. While you want to make sure you're sexually compatible, the first time you have sex with a particular person, it will likely not resemble a porn scene or the fantasy you have in your head. This does not necessarily mean that you're not sexually compatible and that you could not still have stimulating and fulfilling sex with this person for the long term. Often knowing someone a bit more (having some intimate knowledge of him) will increase sexual intimacy and satisfaction. You will not likely have that intimacy with the other guy just after the first date. Also, the nervousness I mentioned earlier that may accompany a first date could interfere with sexual performance for you or him and could get in the way of experiencing a true representation of what sex could be like between the two of you.

I'm not saying that you have to wait until marriage or some milestone in your relationship before having sex; as I mentioned, you may want to know if you're sexually compatible—and as gay men, we have a few more obstacles in our way to figuring this out than our heterosexual counterparts. Just know that if you wait a couple of dates and get to know the person a bit better and are more comfortable with each other, the sex will likely be better and a more accurate representation of your sexual compatibility. Also, if you would like to have safer sex, you will want to discuss sexually transmitted infections, and that will be a lot more likely to happen and be an easier conversation if you're more comfortable with the guy.

Here's a last word of caution about sex on the first date—I promise. For some, there is a strong belief, perhaps even subconsciously, that the best thing you can offer someone is your body and sex. As gay men, a number of us have grown up with a strong sex drive and low self-esteem. Again, this low self-esteem tends to be more prevalent with gay men versus our heterosexual counterparts because of internalized homophobia. Growing up with an increased fear of being rejected by others and the anxiety of having to navigate in a heterosexist world leads to the internalization of negative feelings and thoughts of who we are (Shilo and Savaya 2011). This combination of high sex drive and low self-esteem could lead to using sex to feel better about ourselves, because it provides a sense of worth or value. If you feel that this may be true for you, I strongly suggest you wait at least a few dates before engaging in sex. This will allow you to better understand that you're precious outside of what you're able to offer in the bedroom, or on the couch, or on the kitchen table.

Should There Be a Second Date? (Quiz)

If after the first date you're still unsure if you should have a second date, then use the checklist below to help figure this out. If you have all of the below checked, then he deserves another date. If even one item is not checked, then you should probably move on and let him down politely.

- ☐ So far, he meets more criteria than not on my Traits That Matter Work Sheet.
- ☐ I found him attractive.

- ☐ He was respectful of me and of my time surrounding the date.
- ☐ There is at least a part of me that is excited about/looking forward to spending more time with him.

Your True Love Story: Keeping That First-Date Feeling

Bobby (thirty-nine) and Angel (forty-two)

Together: seven years

When they met in the summer of 2009, Angel was in the middle of some intense dealings with two friends. The two friends were separately relying on him for hours a night, and it was emotionally draining for Angel. In terms of his career, he was at the best place he had ever been professionally and loved where he was working. It had been at least a year since he had been in a relationship. Bobby was not having the same type of work success that Angel was having at the time they met; he was struggling to enjoy the work he was doing. He had been out of a relationship for almost a year, which for him was a longer time than usual to not be in a relationship, but he was making a conscious effort to give himself time to grieve and learn from his past romance.

Bobby and Angel were introduced via e-mail through a mutual friend. She admitted to not knowing whether they were each other's types in terms of attraction but thought they would get along. The two of them e-mailed for a bit, and then Bobby asked if Angel wanted to keep writing or meet up. Angel said he definitely preferred to meet in person than to keep writing with a "stranger." So it was time to set up the first date. It had been a rainy summer, so Bobby suggested that Angel pick outdoor plans, and he would pick indoor plans; depending on the weather, they would partake in whatever plans made sense. Angel found this so clever, cute, and fun.

While each was planning his picks for the date, they took into account what they already knew the other liked. Each of the places they wound up going to that afternoon, evening, and night (yes, it was a long date) were fun for both and conducive to them getting to know each other.

Seven years later, they still look back fondly on that first date as an entry into their current secure, loving, and enjoyable relationship.

Reference

Shilo, G., and R. Savaya. 2011. "Effects of Family and Friend Support on LGB Youths' Mental Health and Sexual Orientation Milestones." *Family Relations* 60 (3): 318–330.

CHAPTER 7
Keep the Dating Momentum Going

Congratulations, you have made it this far—a successful first date that leaves you wanting more. These later dates should not be treated entirely like the first date. While you still want to be respectful and show that you care, you also want to let down your guard a bit and get to know each other in different types of environments and situations. Now instead of working to figure out if he is second-date material, you're looking to see if he is serious-boyfriend material.

Be More Adventurous and More Relaxed

Over the next few dates, try to mix in some more adventurous activities that fit within his and your interests. Along with these more involved dates, you will also want to introduce some downtime at his place and yours; cook a meal, or watch a movie or a show you both enjoy. You want to get an idea of what he is like when the mood is relaxed and he is at your place or in his. Seeing these sides is important in order for you to get as well-rounded a perspective of the guy as possible so that you're making a more informed decision as to whether or not he is meeting your needs and is a match.

Also, try not to have the second through sixth dates be all in the same week. At least a few days between dates (so some time away from him) will allow you space to process what it is really like to be with him and what he is really like. If you're constantly with him or preparing to go on a date with him, you will get wrapped up in dating him, and soon it will just become some habit that you keep doing because you're used to it and not so much because the guy is your match. You also want to make sure that you're living your own life and that neither dating nor this guy is taking it over. It would be beneficial for you to see now how respectful he is able to be of your space and life. I know that you may be head over heels and want to spend as much time as possible together, especially during that beginning (honeymoon) stage, but trust that doing so will get in the way of making an informed decision. The patience and discipline you're able to put forth here in terms of spreading these dates out will help ensure that you're entering a healthy relationship. Remember, you need to be comfortable being single for now, or desperation will cloud your thinking, and you will make poor decisions. It's healthy and fulfilling to continue your regular activities and spend time with your friends in the midst of dating.

Bring in the Friends

Most likely after a few dates, you will start to meet each other's friends. This is a big and exciting step. Seeing who he keeps company with will allow you to learn more about him, and your friends meeting him will allow you to get a perspective from trusted sources as to whether or not this guy is a match.

While you do not want to completely gain your perspective of the guy from the friends he keeps, you're able to get a better understanding of him based on with whom he chooses to spend time. When meeting his friends you want to be yourself and be polite, even if a particular friend is not someone you care for. You want to avoid conflict with his friends for a number of reasons. You do not want to cause a scene; this would be embarrassing for you and not make a good impression with the guy you're dating. Also, if you wind up in a long-term relationship, you will have this discomfort with a friend of his you will likely have to see a lot more in your life. And, lastly, maybe that friend is just having a bad day, and when you meet him the next time, he will not be as bad. Err on the side of giving his friends the benefit of the doubt. He will appreciate it, and you will be better off for it. Along these same lines, you will not want to say anything negative to him about his friends when you first meet them. They could be like family to him, and you want to give the friends a chance and be more secure in your relationship before bringing up, in a nice way, some things about his friends that you do not necessarily care for.

I have shared how friends are able to be helpful when figuring out positive traits, looking to find a guy to date, and getting over a breakup. Friends are also of great value when trying to figure out if you have found a true match. Check in with your friends to see what they think. However, do not just generally ask what they think of him, because that will not likely be as helpful as being more specific about what kind of feedback you're looking to get from them. If you're general in your questions, your friends could either not really say what they think just to be agreeable, or they may wind up listing all the negative things they see in the guy. Neither of these will be of benefit. The first will not help you make an informed decision, and the second could wind up making you resentful toward your friends. To get the most of your friends' observations, you want to let them know that you value their opinions and, without them getting into any details about his traits, you want to know if the guy you're dating seems like a good match for you. Based on seeing the two of you together or hearing about the times you're together, does he seem like someone you could be with long term? If they say they do not see you as a match, you will still want to stay away from finding out their opinions of his traits so that you do not become resentful toward them. Instead, ask what they are seeing happening or what they have heard about how the two of you interact that would lead them to believe that you're not a match. This way the comments will be about the dynamic between you and the guy, not about the guy himself. While your friends are a good resource, keep in mind that their opinions should not be the only evidence used in your decision whether or not to pursue this relationship.

Meet the Parents

When meeting his parents, you're going to take whatever politeness, caring, and safety around conversation topics you put into meeting his friends and take it up a notch. Here you really want to make a good impression. This does not mean to not to be yourself, but make sure you're putting your best self forward. Think of it as similar to what I shared about your first date. You really want to show him and his parents that this is important to you and that you're the type of guy they want to have in their lives. Look to bring a small gift if going to their home. If they're not allergic, then flowers are usually a considerate gift. Or if you know that they drink, then a bottle of wine or a spirit that they enjoy would also be appreciated. If you want to get creative and he has told you enough about his parents to get them something out of the ordinary, then go for it, being very careful not to offend. If they are coming over to your place or his and they do drink, you may want to have one of their favorites on hand. Or you could make sure to put out a snack or dessert that they really enjoy. Also, when it comes to dealing with any nervousness you may have about meeting his parents, know that it's natural to have some anxiety, and try to manage it by reminding yourself of all the great qualities you have to offer them and their son.

When it comes to him meeting your parents, one important thing to remember is that you want to make sure that he is taken care of. You want to help him feel as comfortable as possible for his own sake and so that he is better able to put his best foot forward, allowing your parents to see how great he is. You do not want to spend your night trying to have him impress them, but you do want to make sure that they get a good idea of what he is really like. So while giving him some time alone with one or both of your parents is a nice idea so that they are able to bond a bit, make sure you're communicating with each other around what his needs are—be it less alone time with your parents, an uncomfortable conversation topic, or whether you're comfortable with him bringing up something about the two of you. This communication could happen verbally when the two of you are alone or through body language or facial cues if around your parents. Also, if he has not already indicated that he wants to bring a small gift and you know your parents would appreciate that, then discuss with him something that the two of you will bring or have at either your place or his.

You, of course, may be nervous about him meeting your parents. This is also natural, and what could be helpful with this anxiety is for you to remind yourself that you have done the work so far to make sure this guy is a quality match for you. You want to tell yourself that you're looking for them all to get along instead of yearning for your parents' "approval."

If you stay in a place of not having to impress but just wanting him to come across as his true self, then you will be able to better manage the anxiety. And if you're worried about your parents embarrassing you, you may want to consider a talk with them about boundaries for that first meeting, while also giving them some space to be their true selves—no one ever literally died of embarrassment.

Your First Argument

Arguing is an inevitable part of any healthy romantic relationship. Often when I see couples and ask what sort of relationship they would like to create together, one will say that he does not want to argue. I could see why one might say that. Arguments could put us in a really bad place emotionally and make us think that something is wrong with the relationship. I have to let these clients know that arguing is inevitable and healthy because you're two different people and need to have tension around your own needs, desires, and wishes. In order to be fulfilled as individuals, which is vital to a healthy relationship, you need to be able to express yourself even when your partner sees things differently. The key to lessening the emotional toll and damage to the relationship that arguments are able to cause is to argue in a healthy manner.

Often, when arguing, we wind up just talking at each other instead of actually having a dialogue where we hear what the other is saying and respond to that. Often we do not realize that when arguing, our survival instincts have kicked in because we feel we are being attacked. The parts of your brain responsible for responding to feeling attacked or threatened "are first in the chain of command with respect to survival reflexes, and function to trump all your other needs and wants. They are the agents of war (fighting and running away) and defeat (surrendering and playing dead)" (Tatkin 2011). In an argument, the "fighting" can be screaming at your partner, the "running away" may take the form of leaving the room or home, "surrendering" can be one person just giving in and going with what the other person is saying, and "playing dead" can be stonewalling your partner so that you're no longer responding to him, just staying quiet. I imagine at least one of these survival techniques is familiar to you.

We also tend not to realize that when we are arguing, the emotions we are experiencing are not just about that particular topic but are also influenced by what happened to us that day, a previous fight we had with a partner, or even an issue from our childhood that was triggered by something our partners said or did. Almost always, if one of my clients feels that a nerve is easily touched by his partner, there is something he had to deal with in childhood that makes him extra sensitive to that situation. We have him think back to when he was growing up to see if what he is going through now with his partner is in any way related to an issue from childhood. If so, we work to have him share this realization with his partner, helping the partner to know him in a deeper and more intimate way.

The first step in trying to avoid a lot of this noise that does not need to influence how you respond to your partner is to be aware of it. Be aware that when you begin to argue, your brain is kicking into survival mode and not allowing you to think intelligently in order to allow you to hear your partner and make informed comments. In order to hear each other and argue effectively, you will need to take a timeout, along with some breaths, and then get back to the discussion. I would recommend that the timeout be about twenty minutes in order to get out of survival mode. During that time, you want to check in with yourself around what is going on for you (like issues from childhood or the day you had at work) that may be contributing to this situation, and then share this with your partner. It's so important to actually argue about the topic at hand and how that situation is affecting you, not bring in the frustration of your workday or other topics that may also be bothering you. You want to explain your experience around the situation bothering you while labeling and verbalizing as many feelings as possible. When you share your experience and feelings instead of blaming the other person or making demands on him to change something, then he is less likely to get defensive (go into survival mode), and you're both more likely to have a healthy dialogue around the topic.

You want your arguing to be productive and to eventually help you be even more connected and intimate. This will occur if you do the work to argue in a healthy manner by making use of the above tips to help ensure focus on a dialogue that will allow thorough sharing about each other's experience of a situation.

Thriving Past Date One (Quiz)

Are you putting in the work needed to keep the dating momentum going past date one? As you were able to see from this chapter, it takes a good deal of effort to truly maximize the enjoyment and learning when dating. However, when you put in the energy, you get closer to securing your entry into a healthy long-term relationship. You will want to have every box checked below to know that you're on the right track when it comes to navigating this beginning phase of dating.

- ☐ Dates after the first include a mix of more adventurous outings than the first date and relaxed time at home.
- ☐ I'm allowing myself time between dates to do what I normally would and see my friends and family.

- ☐ I know to be on my best behavior with his friends, giving them the benefit of the doubt when first meeting them.
- ☐ When asking my friends what they think about my guy, I will let them know that I'm more interested in whether they see us as a match than I am in their opinions about his traits.
- ☐ When meeting the parents, I will put my best foot forward, showing this is important to me.
- ☐ When he meets my parents, I would want to help him impress while still being true to himself.
- ☐ I accept that we will argue, but I understand there are ways to disagree with each other that are healthy.
- ☐ When arguing, we will work to get out of survival mode and share our experiences so that we are able to truly hear and learn about each other.

Your True Love Story: The Importance of Family—Warts and All
Ross (fifty-seven) and Randy (fifty-three)

Together: thirty years

Family played a vital role from the very beginning of Ross and Randy's relationship. Ross's cousin had a gay roommate she wanted to hook him up with, so she planned a dinner in order for them to get to know each other. As an afterthought, she invited a friend, Randy, to even out the dinner table.

Ross thought the roommate was a nice guy, but he was not Ross's type. Ross and Randy wound up hitting it off though, joking around a lot that night. A few weeks later, the group of four got together again to see a dance performance. This allowed Ross and Randy to get to know each other better, and after about four weeks, they decided to start officially dating.

Soon after dating, Ross joined Randy on a trip home; Randy needed a haircut and really only trusted one person with his hair. Randy warned Ross that his family was "very New England," and a part of this meant everyone had to be very polite. Unfortunately for Ross, this applied to everything, even having to eat what you were served. It just so happened that the night they were with the family, Yankee pot roast was being served. Ross had yet to share with Randy that he had been a strict vegetarian for years. This obviously meant trouble for Ross as he wanted to be "polite" and impress Randy's parents, but, unfortunately, his body was no longer producing the enzymes needed to process meat. What did Ross do in this situation? Not wanting to begin his relationship with Randy's family on a bad note, he ate the pot roast—and paid the price. Ross spent the next two days in the bathroom, horrified that the family must have been wondering why Randy would date a guy who had to spend so much time in someone else's bathroom.

Likely unrelated to the bathroom situation, Randy's mother was resistant to accepting Ross. This was because she struggled with coming to terms with her son being with another man. Two years after meeting, when they married, Randy's mother refused to attend the wedding. However, his mother got a second chance. They were married again, twenty-one years after the first wedding, and Randy's mother called him to say that she would like to attend, and she admitted that not going to his first wedding was one of the greatest mistakes of her life.

Ross's side of the family also had difficulty accepting their gay son and Randy. When Ross came out, his parents did not speak to him for five years. When he made them aware that he was getting married, there was no reply from his parents. Randy, valuing family such a great deal, decided to reach out to Ross's parents, writing notes and trying to include them but to no avail.

Ross knew that his mother had come around when she invited them over and taught them how to play bridge. This was significant because for her, bridge was a game that you only taught couples to play. Another symbol of her acceptance was letting them know that she wanted to help them with a down payment for their condo. Ross knew this was significant because he was aware that her thinking was that if you owned property together, that was marriage, and there she was, helping to make that possible.

The shift toward acceptance from Ross's father came when they were in the same room (for the first time in years) at Ross's uncle's funeral. Ross's aunt told her brother to get over his not being accepting, as being gay was not a phase. On that day, his father began speaking with Ross and Randy. He was not all that comfortable, but he did engage with them. Later, Ross's father was able to show his acceptance more. One year when he visited for Thanksgiving (the year Ross's mother had died), he let them know that before anything, they were all going to have to go to Ikea. They made the trip, and he took them to the dining room section and told them to pick out a kitchen table. He explained that the kitchen table is where homework is done with the children, where the family eats breakfast, where the couple argues about who is going to pay the bills, and where the couple drinks a glass of wine at 2:00 a.m. and figures out how they are going to get their kids through school. He was letting them know that any good family has a good kitchen table, and he was seeing them as a family. That table has been with Ross and Randy for a decade. The dogs have chewed legs, one of the kids drew on it with a fork, and it has plenty of nicks.

For Ross and Randy, from the beginning, inclusion of each other's family was important and helped them create their own healthy relationship and family. Like that beat-up kitchen table, Ross and Randy feel it's vital to embrace family—"warts and all."

Reference

Tatkin, S. 2011. *Wired for Love: How Understanding Your Partner's Brain and Attachment Style Can Help You Defuse Conflict and Build a Secure Relationship.* Oakland, CA: New Harbinger Publications, Inc.

CHAPTER 8
Sex—Let's Talk about It

Sex for gay men is definitely different from sex in the straight world—not only because there tend to be a lot fewer vaginas in gay sex, but there are also a host of variables related to gay sex that most straight men do not have to deal with. I'm going to cover many of them in this chapter in hopes of having you enjoy amazing sexual experiences.

Let's Get the Sexually Transmitted Infections (STI) Talk out of the Way

I could not ethically have a chapter on sex and not discuss STIs. First, you may be asking why I'm using the term STIs and not STDs. STI is a more accurate description of what can be transmitted through sex because not all sexually transmitted infections actually become a "disease." I also feel that the word "infection" is less stigmatizing than "disease."

If you want to be responsible about your health and the health of the guy you're dating, then there are some basic aspects of STIs that you should explore and commit to. The first is to make sure you know which infections are able to be transmitted sexually; how they are transmitted, prevented, and treated; and what the symptoms are, if any. A reliable source for this information is the Centers for Disease Control and Prevention (cdc.gov). You will also want to speak with your doctor about your sexual activity and learn from him or her how often you should be tested for STIs. I understand that it may not be comfortable to speak with your doctor about your sex life, but it's a must. You will have to "bite the bullet" and let the doctor know what else you like to "bite."

If you become infected, I strongly recommend that, in addition to getting treatment, you discuss this with the guy you're dating. You will have to figure out if he needs treatment as well and discuss how you will have sex moving forward. If you're practicing monogamy and an infidelity is discovered because of the STI, this does not necessarily have to spell the end of your relationship. A lot of relationships stay healthy even after cheating occurs. You will want to have a thorough dialogue about the infidelity so that you're each able to understand what occurred and why and how you're able to move forward to rebuild trust. If this does not seem possible, then ending the relationship may be your best option. Another option is discussing whether or not monogamy makes sense for the two of you. I will discuss this in more detail later.

I do not know a ton of men who actually like to wear condoms. While understanding that condoms add a level of safety to sex (though there are still STI risks involved in any sex, even with condoms), some gay men prefer to have sex without them. Some of these men have decided to use preexposure prophylaxis (PrEP). At the time that I'm writing this, PrEP has been shown, if taken as prescribed, to dramatically reduce the chances of HIV- men becoming infected with HIV. PrEP does not provide any level of protection from any other STIs. I'm not saying whether or not I think you should use PrEP; I just want to make sure that you're aware that it is an option. If having this preventive medication does interest you, then I would suggest learning more about it and then speaking with your doctor, who will have to provide you with a prescription.

The final notes I will make here about STIs are about discordant couples, in which one partner is HIV- and the other is HIV+. If you're the one in the relationship who is HIV+, I recommend you disclose that status to the guy you're dating before you start engaging in sex (regardless of the level of viral load), as all sex involves some risk. Please know that many HIV- men are open to having relationships with HIV+ men, especially those who are adhering to their medication regimen and are undetectable in terms of the virus. If you're the one who is HIV-, know that there are precautions you're able to take to lower your risk, including PrEP, that would allow for you to fully enjoy sex. Also know that sometimes you can be at less risk of becoming infected with HIV if in a monogamous relationship with someone who is HIV+ because you know what you're dealing with and so are already taking measures accordingly. An alternative to this is possibly putting yourself at risk if you're dating someone who is HIV-, and then he cheats and converts to being HIV+ without your knowledge, and you're not protecting yourself accordingly. I suggest usually being open and honest about STIs, as there are ways to have pleasurable sex and healthy relationships while managing them.

To Be or Not to Be...Monogamous

This is an issue that tends to come up more among gay couples than straight. Our community is not as tied to the concept that one has to only have sex with one's partner. A study of same-sex male couples showed that 42 percent had arrangements that were nonmonogamous (Parsons, Starks, DuBois, Grov, and Golub 2013).

Whether you want monogamy or an open relationship is something that you will have to each decide on your own and then figure out together. When I reference an open relationship in this book, I'm also referring to the option of polyamory. It's important that you each figure out separately what you're looking for from the relationship and what role sex and intimate emotions will play in that. If you decide that you cannot have your needs met in the relationship if there is something happening outside of just the two of you, then monogamy would make the most sense for you to discuss. If you decide that you can get what you need out of your primary relationship while still having sex or intimate relationships with others and allowing him to do the same, then you may want to have dialogue about an open relationship. Going the nonmonogamous route will take some work, including being aware of increased risk of STIs, managing emotions that will come up, figuring out if there will be parameters around what is happening outside the relationship, and if so, what those parameters will be and if you will be open to changing them over time. In a study comparing monogamous and nonmonogamous relationships, it was found that the gay male couples that were in open relationships "appeared to maintain healthy and satisfying primary relationships" (LaSala 2004).

How to Have Mind-Blowing Sex

My first tip is to have plenty of lube. My second tip is to talk openly about sex with the guy you're dating. Regardless of how frequently gay men are stereotyped as beings who voraciously and constantly hunger to hook up, sex can still be an especially difficult area for us to be open and honest about—to ourselves and the person with whom we are having sex. This is partly due to the general stigma around sex as being something naughty that you do in the privacy of your home with the lights out. This shame around sex is compounded for gay men because for a lot of us, being gay was experienced as confusing and negative, so sex with other men might have been interpreted as wrong or bad (Iasenza 2010).

We need to get rid of the unrealistic stigma around sex and explore and talk about what gives us pleasure. Do you enjoy spanking? Rimming? Golden showers? Masturbating? Blowjobs? Needle play? Fisting? As long as you're with a consenting adult, there need be no shame in your game. You deserve to experience what you enjoy, so talk with your guy about your preferences, and see what is able to happen between the two of you or with others.

Not sure what you like? This is the case for most of us, and even when we figure out what we like, that may change over time. To figure out what you're currently into, it would be helpful to recall your past peak sexual experiences and biggest turn-ons (Morin 1995). You may also get some information by paying attention to your fantasies. What images tend to enter your mind when you're thinking about being stimulated? What do you imagine doing or having done to you that gets you aroused? What have you always wanted to try?

To have mind-blowing sex, we need to respect ourselves—even if we temporarily suspend the concept of respect for sexual role pay. One area specific to gay men concerning lack of respect is bottom shaming. While bottoming may not actually be enjoyed by some gay men, a lot of gay men would take pleasure in it but deprive themselves of it because of bottom shaming. As discussed earlier in this book, as gay men, we place an unnecessary high value on masculinity in order to feel better about ourselves. Bottoming is seen by some men as being feminine or being the "female" in the relationship because in the heterosexual world, it's the woman who is traditionally penetrated. Unfortunately, because our society tends to see women in an unjust way, this association with women equates to being weak and less than. If you think you would like to bottom, I suggest you own wanting that stimulation and pleasure, and allow yourself to bottom. Doing so could show how secure you are in your gender and sexuality.

Grooming

To manscape or not to manscape? That is the question. While the truth is that most men (gay or straight) prefer a partner groomed around the genitals, not all men do. If the guy you're dating has mentioned at some point that he prefers a partner who is groomed, and you're comfortable with it, then go for it. Or if you prefer to be au natural, and he is into that, then fantastic; your life was made just a bit easier. If the two of you are on different pages in terms of how you like to keep your body and how he likes his partners, you will have one of your first dialogues and attempts at compromise. You will have to figure out why it's important for you to groom or not groom and share this with him, with him sharing why he prefers what he does. Hopefully, through this honest dialogue, you will be able to problem solve so that you both get some sort of win out of the situation.

You, of course, also get to state your preference when it comes to his manscaping. If you know you have a preference, make sure to bring it up in conversation, and see how he feels about your preference. If you're not sure if you want him to manscape, you may want to ask him what he prefers, and wait to see what it's like to have sex with him the way he chooses to groom. If it works for you, then you're set. If it does not, then a dialogue around preferences will need to be had here—again, you share and problem solve so that you each get some sort of win out of the discussion.

Love the Skin You're In

Earlier in the book, I mention that online, on television, and in movies and magazines, we get bombarded by images of what signifies beauty and what we are supposed to desire. These images tend to be young people with ridiculously maintained bodies. Gay men seem to be especially susceptible to believing that our bodies need to look a certain way.

A study of gay and bisexual men showed that, more than heterosexual men, they seemed to desire a more muscular body with low body fat because being single longer than their straight counterparts meant they wanted to appear younger longer to be appealing to attractive men (Chaney 2008). Gay men also tend to be overly focused on body image due to having a greater need than our heterosexual counterparts for external validation. Many of us grew up with shame around who we were internally, so we stayed away from exploring our inner selves and instead focused on external accomplishments and getting recognition and validation for these (Downs 2012). A fixation on outward appearance is a perfect example of how we would look to get validation for something external instead of validation for who we are as people. Not all gay men fall into this trap, but growing up with such shame does lead a lot of gay men to be obsessed with perfecting their external physical features.

Having a negative perception of your body could lead to lack of participating in or enjoying sex. If you feel that this is the case for you, you may want to see a psychotherapist to properly work through issues related to feeling you need to look a certain way to attract other men or get validation. You will want to find a therapist who has familiarity with gay culture so that he or she is better able to understand how you grew up and the environment you're currently in that is putting such pressure on you to look a certain way.

Are You Ready for Hot Sex? (Quiz)

Now let's see if you're in a place to begin to have hot sex with the guy you're dating. You will want to be able to honestly check all six boxes in order to maximize your enjoyment of sex in the relationship.

- ☐ I know what infections are transmitted sexually; how they are transmitted, prevented, and treated; and what the symptoms are, if any.
- ☐ I commit to telling my guy if I get an STI.
- ☐ We have come to a decision on whether or not to be monogamous based on individual thinking and talking together on the matter.
- ☐ I have given thought to what I really like about sex (removing any stigmas) and have shared this with the guy I'm dating.
- ☐ I know how I feel about grooming and have discussed with the guy I'm dating what will happen around grooming.
- ☐ If I feel I have body issues keeping me from sex, I will seek out a therapist who has experience working with gay men.

Your True Love Story: When It Comes to Sex, Let It All Hang Out
Kurt (forty-two) and Brian (forty)

Together: ten years

Kurt was thirty-two when he and Brian became roommates. They had been friends beforehand. At this time, Kurt was not in a place where he was seeking a relationship. He was very comfortable being single, but as he continued to room with Brian, he slowly started to realize that he was falling in love with him. For Kurt, this was frightening and something he didn't feel ready for.

When Brian became Kurt's roommate, he was thirty years old and in one of those moments in life when he was evaluating what was going on in his life and what was ahead for him. He was also at this time very comfortable being single. He was not looking for a relationship and was extremely career driven. He was hyper focused and spending a lot of time working on a large professional endeavor. Even in the midst of all this, Brian was able to see that he was developing feelings for Kurt.

Those early feelings blossomed into a thriving and fulfilling ten-year (and counting) relationship. The constant feeling of being so loved and loving someone else so completely is one of the more special aspects of their relationship for Kurt. He feels that he does not have this in a lot of parts of his life. Kurt feels that in ten years, they have managed to build a relationship where he can stand before Brian and tell him absolutely anything—the worst things and the hardest things—and it's OK. He does not experience that sense of home and safety anywhere else in the world.

What Brian appreciates most about their relationship is the fact that it provides for him stability and consistency. He cherishes the ability to share his life and life experiences with someone he cares deeply about and loves and to be equally interested in someone else's life and experiences. To have that "rock"—to feel fully loved for successes and failures, his good side and bad side, his healthy days and unhealthy days—is so powerful, life changing, and beyond what Brian thought possible.

These concepts of being fully loved and there for each other are evident when they share the work they have done toward making their sex life more fulfilling. Kurt sees sex as an ever-evolving part of their relationship, having gone through periods of not having sex at all with each other and periods when they were both very interested in having sex with each other—and having gone through these cycles more than once throughout their ten years. Like most couples, they learned that there is not always an equal desire to have sex with the other at the same time and that this can lead to discomfort and pain. When they each have gotten over these initial feelings related to rejection, which is foreign to them because they do not reject each other in other areas of their relationship, then they are able to have a real moment for reevaluation. They communicate about what is happening and how it relates to what they are unhappy about surrounding sex or the relationship in general.

For Brian, they hit "rock bottom" in terms of sex within their relationship at a point when they just stopped having sex. They were both angry about it for different reasons, and there was no communication at all about sex. Brian admits that it was mostly his shutting down that drove the lack of communication, and this led to a lot of resentment and anger on Kurt's end. This behavior was a violation of being able to be vulnerable with each other. When they started to talk about how they were feeling and what they wanted when it came to sex, especially Brian working to tap into his own vulnerability and put himself in front of Kurt regarding sex, they realized how much their sex life and relationship improved. Now continued dialogue about sex is a must for Kurt and Brian.

References

Downs, A. 2012. *The Velvet Rage: Overcoming the Pain of Growing Up Gay in a Straight Man's World*. Boston, MA: Da Capo Press.

Chaney, M. P. 2008. "Muscle Dysmorphia, Self-esteem, and Loneliness among Gay and Bisexual Men." *International Journal of Men's Health* 7 (2): 157–170.

Iasenza, S. 2010. "What Is Queer About Sex?: Expanding Sexual Frames in Theory and Practice." *Family Process* 49 (3): 291–308.

Morin, J. 1995. *The Erotic Mind: Unlocking the Inner Sources of Sexual Passion and Fulfillment*. New York, NY: HarperCollins Publishers.

Parsons, J. T., T. J. Starks, S. DuBois, C. Grov, and S. A. Golub. 2013. "Alternatives to Monogamy Among Gay Male Couples in a Community Survey: Implications for Mental Health and Sexual Risk." *Archives of Sexual Behavior* 42: 303–312.

CHAPTER 9
Things Are Getting Serious

By this point, the two of you have been on a lot of dates—some casual, some more adventurous. You likely also have met each other's friends and parents and have had sex. Getting to this point is quite exciting, and you should be proud of what you have accomplished thus far. Now let's talk about moving the relationship to the next level.

Just the Toothbrush?

While the toothbrush is a small, innocuous item that one would think could cause no harm to a relationship, it has been known to start many fights and cause hurt feelings. When you feel ready to leave a toothbrush at his place and have him leave one at yours, talk about it; don't just surprise him with it. At this point, you're definitely learning about each other, but do not assume that you know how he would feel about taking this step without asking him. Some men do feel that this is a big step, as it shows a level of commitment and connection to have something at the other person's place. If you're ready for this step, then chances are that he is, too. If he happens not to be, that's OK. There's no need to go running for the hills and end the relationship. Talk about each of your needs and wants when it comes to each other's places. You will want to have this same type of dialogue when it comes to leaving clothes at each other's places.

Even when your clothes and toiletries are at his place, be careful not to spend too many nights together. You're not living together just yet, for good reason. You will read more about moving in together later in this chapter.

Handling Disagreements

With the increased amount of time you will be spending together and as you start to replace fantasy with the reality of what he's really like, there will be arguing. This is natural and healthy for you two as individuals. In building healthy relationships, we need to make sure we stay differentiated as individuals, being aware of our own needs, wishes, dreams, and perspectives. And we want to be able to share these needs, wishes, dreams, and perspectives with our guys and for them to do the same.

An added barrier that two men have when it comes to dealing with disagreements is our resistance to being vulnerable. It takes vulnerability to share your needs, wishes, and dreams as well as to take responsibility and admit when you were wrong and apologizing. Gay men may have more difficulty being vulnerable, especially with other men, because many of us are trying to prove that we are not needy or too emotional in order to adhere to the masculine stereotype strongly reinforced as preferred by most of society (Greenan and Tunnell 2003).

So how do you allow yourself to be more vulnerable? The first step is to become aware that what may be holding you back from opening up to your guy is not a need to actually protect yourself now but instead some leftover childhood need or coping skill that is only getting in the way of you building intimacy with your partner.

> As children we found ways to protect ourselves from vulnerability, from being hurt, diminished, and disappointed. We put on armor; we used our thoughts, emotions, and behaviors as weapons; and we learned how to make ourselves scarce, even to disappear. Now as adults we realize that to live with courage, purpose, and connection—to be the person whom we long to be—we must again be vulnerable. We must take off the armor, put down the weapons, show up, and let ourselves be seen. (Brown 2012)

To further help with vulnerability and intimacy building, you will also want to start questioning held beliefs about having to be masculine and whether or not you believe that having and sharing feelings equate to weakness. Hopefully you will realize that you need not fit society's stereotype of masculinity and that being vulnerable is showing great strength.

So when a disagreement occurs, be open to sharing your experience and feelings around that situation and to caring and being curious about what his experience and feelings are around the situation. Listen to each other, and be aware that you're two different people who experience the same situation differently. You will know each other better and, for those issues that are solvable, create solutions in which you both wind up winning. I make a point of saying "those issues that are solvable" because not all relationship problems are solvable. Some problems are based on differences that are so ingrained in one's personality or needs that they cannot be solved, and what matters with these types of issues is to be able to have an ongoing dialogue around them (Gottman 1999). An ongoing dialogue will allow you to better understand what is happening for each other around this issue and to better cope with the fact that the issue is not going to be solved but instead will be something that the two of you will live and work with as a team.

Moving In

You have stuff at each other's places. The sex is hot. You're enjoying each other's company. You have learned how to argue effectively. Maybe it's time to move in together? Before discussing the topic with him, you will want to gauge (1) how strong the relationship is up until this point, (2) where you're able to see it going, and (3) what your gut is telling you. Let's talk further about each of these topics.

There is evidence that when you start dating someone new, you have an increase in energy and focus on that person due to changes in some of the chemicals in your brain—elevated levels of dopamine and norepinephrine and lower levels of serotonin (Fisher, Aron, Mashek, Li, and Brown 2002). This helps to explain the feeling of butterflies in your stomach when you think of him or see him. Hours apart from each other could feel like days. You find yourself getting stimulated just by thinking about the two of you having sex. This is natural and comes courtesy of the chemicals just mentioned. If during the beginning stages (that are supposed to be mostly bliss), you find yourself having consistent problems with the guy you're dating, then you will likely be better off moving on. Things do not have to be perfect between the two you; there will be some bumps, even in the beginning. However, you should not have to consistently be dealing with issues of incompatibility when first dating. If at least once a week you're arguing and having trouble making the relationship work, then you need to end that relationship, grieve that loss, and decide when you want to continue to date again.

Along these same lines, early on you want to be aware of the one emotion that you must not tolerate: contempt. Contempt is a very strong feeling that someone is beneath you. You will never be able to build a healthy relationship if you do not each feel that the person you're with is a worthy partner—someone to whom you're willing to listen, respect, and with whom you could work out life's issues. Occasional arguments, even early in dating, are fine, natural, and expected. However, if you're picking up on a belief from either one of you that the other person is insignificant and not worthy of respect, the dating needs to end, and you need to move on out of respect for yourself and your TME. Studies have shown that out of all the behaviors that occur when a long-term couple is arguing, contempt is the one that will get in the way of being able to repair from an argument and ultimately having a successful relationship (Gottman 1999).

What you do want at the beginning is to feel at peace with your partner. You want to feel some sense of safety. And you want to feel like you have the potential to be yourself in front of your potential mate. These feelings are a strong foundation for a lasting and fulfilling relationship. The expectation is not that you will feel these three things fully right away, nor is that likely; however, you should experience the beginnings of these feelings early on in the time you're spending with this person.

In the beginning stages of dating, you should also be assessing whether or not this is a guy for whom you would be willing to do the work it takes to stay in a relationship—especially once the positive chemicals I just mentioned level off. All long-term relationships require work in order to make them remain stimulating and worthwhile, no matter how compatible and in love you may be. To figure out if this is a guy you would want to do the work to keep a long-term relationship with, use your Traits That Matter Work Sheet to see if he is still meeting your needs. Also, remind yourself of your positive traits to make sure that he is still a guy who is worthy of all you have to offer. If all of this is still on target, then you're on the right track and should consider continuing the relationship.

Another tool to help you know if you're on the right track is your gut. I'm sure you have heard people say that when making decisions, you should pay attention to your gut. Well, they were steering you in the right direction. Your intestines actually have a network of nerves that send information to your brain, so they can be relied upon to help you make decisions (Siegel 2011). While you shouldn't blindly just follow your gut, it's definitely worth pausing in order to consider what it has to "say."

Along the same lines of paying attention to your gut, I find that feelings in general are undervalued in terms of how they are able to properly inform important decisions. Often, I have heard people say not to let feelings get in the way. These people are wrong. You should pay attention to what your feelings are telling you. The emotional part of our brains has been around longer than the rational part of our brains and therefore is more evolved and in many cases has the ability to make quality decisions more easily and quickly than the rational part (Lehrer 2010). Feelings should not always be our deciding factor, but they deserve to at least be paid attention to. Here I will remind you how to pay attention to your feelings. In your mind, recall the situation you're dealing with, and then tune into your body and notice what is happening. Are you feeling tightness in your chest? Are you experiencing heaviness on your shoulders? Is there a cramping in your stomach? Whatever you feel, you should stay with it and lean into it, label the emotion behind the physical feeling, and see what that feeling would like for you to do (Frederick 2009). You're making an important decision when figuring out whether or not to continue in a relationship with someone, so you want to make sure to use as many effective resources as possible, including your actual feelings about the guy and the situation.

If after taking the time and care to work through figuring out if living together makes sense for your relationship, you decide that it does, then there is a lot to decide during your discussions on moving in. The first will be determining where you will live. The best decision for the relationship would be to start at a new place, not your place or his. This is ideal because if you move into one of your places, it will still feel like that person's and not your place together. Also, one of you would automatically have to do a lot more adjusting than the other (to a new space, neighborhood, and neighbors), and this could put a slight to large strain on the relationship. Even the person whose place it is would have to adjust to someone else living in his space.

If you're moving into a new place, some of what you will each individually want to figure out is what neighborhoods you like, what kinds of spaces you would like to live in, how much you want to spend a month for the space and utilities, and how close you want to be to a downtown area. Then you will share your lists of wants with each other and try to come to a compromise where you both win.

If it's not possible to move into a new place together, that does not mean your relationship is doomed or one of you will never be truly comfortable; it just means a bit more adjusting for each of you. Below is a list of other topics you will want to be sure to cover before the move happens.

- How will cleaning be divided, or will you split the cost of a cleaning service?
- How will household chores (like grocery shopping and cooking) be managed?
- How will bills be split?
- Will you have a joint bank account or credit card to pay for shared expenses?
- What will be your policy on having friends over, including staying over?
- Do you want pets? If so, which and how many?

Here is my advice on some of the issues above. If you have not already lived with a boyfriend, you may be surprised to know how much resentment can build up over household cleaning and chores. Trouble arises when one or both of you feel you're doing more to clean up the place, someone does not clean up to the level that the other would like, one of you does not clean in a timely enough manner, or one of you is home more and is expected to take on more of the household chores. I highly recommend, if you're able, to get a cleaning service to take care of your place. This will be one of the best investments in the relationship you will ever make. If this is not an option, then I would suggest you set up a chart for the chores, deciding who is responsible for what, and have it somewhere you could both easily see it. You also will want to decide if you prefer to rotate chores or always be responsible for the same chores.

Finances are another issue that could put a strain on a relationship. To help reduce some of this strain early on, you may want to consider a shared credit card that you use for shared expenses, such as items for your home, eating out, and traveling. This tends to work well because no one has to worry about paying anyone back; you just each separately pay half when the bill comes. Plus, you get the bonus of reward points or cash back that you could use together. Another aspect of the financial piece that you will want to establish before you live together is whether larger household items such as rent, mortgage, or vehicles will be split evenly or based on income. Remember, when deciding your own preference, realize that the financial situation between the two of you (such as who is making more) may change in the future.

Yes, puppies are adorable. Puppies also are a lot of work and a huge long-term financial, temporal, and emotional responsibility. Before getting a pet together, truly think about what it would mean for your lifestyle and your relationship. Pets in general are healthy for individuals and relationships; you just need to be sure that you and your relationship are ready to introduce another living being that will need to be fed, watched, walked, taken to the vet, cared for when sick, and grieved for if the relationship ends. I recommend living together for at least a year before deciding on a pet. This will give you and your guy time to learn more about each other and what it would be like to have a pet while living together and further time and evidence to assess whether or not this is a relationship that will last long-term.

Pop the Question?

After living together for a couple of years and feeling that you're in a healthy relationship, you may wonder if it's time to get married. This decision has the ability to be a bit loaded for gay men. Some feel that marriage is a heterosexual institution that we need not fit into. Others feel that it's a basic right that we deserved, and now that we have it in the United States, we should take full advantage of the benefits that come with it. If your thinking is along the lines of the former, then I would suggest, for the health of the relationship, that you do have some anniversary that you make sure to celebrate each year. If you're pro marriage and feel that this guy is someone you could commit to long term, then go for it. But before you do, there is one big topic that you need to agree on first. If you have not already, you need to agree on whether or not you want children and, if so, how many and through what means (surrogate, adoption, etc.). What I mentioned for that cute puppy pales in comparison to what you will have to be responsible for if having a child. Be smart. Make sure that if you want children, you want them for the right reasons (not just to fulfill some "preferred" heterosexual image or prove anything to anyone) and are ready to love and care for them no matter how they turn out.

If you will be the one popping the question, then I recommend trying to get an idea of what he would truly appreciate as a proposal. Do not get caught up in what you would like or what they do in the movies if this is not what he would want. If you really want to be the one asked, then I would suggest that you discuss this with him, letting him know that you're interested in marriage and like the idea of being proposed to. I would recommend stopping there (short of telling him how to propose to you) in order to allow for some romance and for him to feel some autonomy.

Could This Be What I Was Looking For? (Quiz)

Wow, this is a major chapter. We have you living together and possibly getting married. Before taking either of those major steps, let's get an idea if you're truly ready. You will want to have all of these checked below in order to increase your chances of success at taking the final steps in setting up a healthy long-term relationship.

- ☐ I'm aware of the possibility that I may be unnecessarily putting up a wall around my emotions, and, if so, the relationship and I would be better served by being vulnerable.
- ☐ I understand that with a disagreement, we are able to both win if we truly listen to each other's experience and do not look to problem solve right away.
- ☐ I know that some problems between us are not solvable, and the best way to handle these issues is to have an ongoing dialogue about them.
- ☐ I feel at peace, secure, and myself most of the time when I'm with him.
- ☐ It seems that I would do the work necessary to make the relationship thrive if we were to enter something long term.
- ☐ It seems that he would do the work necessary to make the relationship thrive if we were to enter something long term.
- ☐ When listening to my gut and feelings, they are letting me know that I'm on the right course in dating this guy.
- ☐ There is no contempt present in the current relationship.
- ☐ I have taken care to discuss the issues recommended discussing before moving in together.

Your True Love Story: Talk Like Your Love Depends on It

Fitz (fifty-two) and Oliver (forty-four)

Together: nine years

When Fitz and Oliver met, Fitz was two years into a career change. He had recently completed graduate school and was a bit disillusioned in his new career because he was working so much and was not seeing the financial payoff. At this time, Fitz had been single for a long time and was not focused on finding a partner. He was actually planning on moving away from the East Coast, where he was living at the time. But meeting Oliver led to a change of plans.

They met at an ongoing gay-themed event at the time. Fitz enjoyed it because while it was "cruisey," it was a "friendly cruise fest" with a brotherly feel and a sense of belonging to a nurturing community.

After they met, things moved pretty quickly, with Fitz really being into Oliver and intensely pursuing him—perhaps too intensely, because Oliver wound up feeling overwhelmed and broke up with him. But after five days, he realized that he had made a mistake and called Fitz to start dating again.

At about a year and some months into their relationship, Fitz was made aware of a serious family health issue that required him to go out of state. At this time, Oliver was about to go back to school and was looking forward to some time to relax before starting a vigorous academic endeavor. He decided that he was not going to accompany Fitz to see his family and help him through this ordeal. This was difficult for Fitz to accept because he expected Oliver to be there for him around this issue. This could have been a breaking point for the couple. Instead, they were able to do some self-reflecting and share with each other their own experiences of the situation.

Through this work, Oliver was able to see that he had not truly learned skills to deal with what Fitz was going through, and he was scared. And

Fitz was able to begin to accept what Oliver was going through and that the two of them were just not yet at a place in their relationship where he could expect Oliver to support him in the way he was hoping. Oliver did not wind up going with Fitz. They processed this issue for a few years and were able to get to a place of complete acceptance and understanding around where the relationship and each of them were at the time. This effort has been key in allowing them to continue their exciting and healthy relationship for almost ten years.

References

Brown, B. 2012. *Daring Greatly: How the Courage to Be Vulnerable Transforms the Way We Live, Love, Parent and Lead.* New York, NY: Gotham Books.

Fisher, H. E., A. Aron, D. Mashek, H. Li, and L. L. Brown. 2002. "Defining the Brain Systems of Lust, Romantic Attraction, and Attachment." *Archives of Sexual Behavior* 31.5: 413–9.

Frederick, R. J. 2009. *Living Like You Mean It: Use the Wisdom and Power of Your Emotions to Get the Life You Really Want.* San Francisco, CA: Jossey-Bass.

Gottman, J. M. 1999. *The Marriage Clinic: A Scientifically-Based Marital Therapy.* New York, NY: W. W. Norton & Company Inc.

Greenan, D. E. and G. Tunnell. 2003. *Couple Therapy With Gay Men.* New York, NY: The Guilford Press.

Lehrer, J. 2010. *How We Decide.* New York, NY: First Mariner Books.

Siegel, D. J. 2011. *Mindsight: The New Science of Personal Transformation.* New York, NY: Bantam Books.

CHAPTER 10
Final Words of Advice and Encouragement

By the time you get through this book, you will realize that for us, entering a healthy relationship is not like it is in the movies, love songs, or romantic novels we grew up on and continue to experience, especially because they tend to focus on a man and a woman. Even if they were telling the story of two guys, they are not reflective of how real life works. It's pleasant and healthy to allow those messages to encourage fantasies and occasional escape, but we need to also stay grounded in the reality that we are not going to lose glass shoes that our Prince Charmings will find and bring back to us. We are likely not going to have the guy next door realize we were meant to be together this entire time and come ring our doorbell. Getting into a relationship that will be lasting, stimulating, and healthy takes work. It takes being very discerning about who deserves your TME, knowing what will truly make you happy in a relationship, and then being strategic about how you meet him and progress in the relationship. Did I just emphasize being strategic when looking for love? Yes. The alternative is sort of like taking a nap and hoping your true love will realize you're "the one," break down your door, and wake you with a kiss. Very sweet. Very never going to happen.

While there can be no guarantees when it comes to finding a person with whom you could be in a long-term, healthy relationship, following the steps in this book will greatly increase your chances. Just doing the work of not being desperate and improving your self-esteem will have you feeling better about yourself, and you'll be more attractive to others—remember, confidence is sexy. Couple that with putting yourself in proper situations to meet the right guys for you, and you're likely to have extremely qualified dating candidates. Follow that through with successful initial dating, and work on figuring out if the relationship should continue, and you're on your way to having something more meaningful than a love song: your own real-life love story.

If you're sincerely working at these steps and still having trouble, you may need to bring in the assistance of a therapist or coach. He or she could help you figure out why you're stuck on any of the steps and give you the personalized guidance that may be necessary. It will likely be worth the extra effort to look for a therapist or coach who has worked with LGBT individuals, as there are nuances to our experiences, especially when it comes to relationships and dating, that will be better understood and worked through by someone with experience helping gay men.

Lastly, I would like to further emphasize the importance of friends. I have mentioned friends as an important resource at various places throughout the book. Let me add to this that friends are also vital in order to keep you sane and enjoying life while you're looking for love and to keep you grounded and fulfilled when starting to date. Even when you start dating and enter into a relationship with your match, you will need your friends to nourish the parts of you that he is not able to, and you will need enriching times with friends to balance out what you're not getting from your romantic relationship. The intimacy you share with your friends will always be a vital part of your life that you deserve.

With or without a romantic relationship, always know that you are precious.

REFERENCES

Brown, B. 2012. *Daring Greatly: How the Courage to Be Vulnerable Transforms the Way We Live, Love, Parent, and Lead.* New York, NY: Gotham Books.

Chaney, M. P. 2008. "Muscle Dysmorphia, Self-esteem, and Loneliness among Gay and Bisexual Men." *International Journal of Men's Health* 7 (2): 157–170.

Downs, A. 2012. *The Velvet Rage: Overcoming the Pain of Growing Up Gay in a Straight Man's World.* Boston, MA: Da Capo Press.

Fisher, H. E., A. Aron, D. Mashek, H. Li, and L. L. Brown. 2002. "Defining the Brain Systems of Lust, Romantic Attraction, and Attachment." *Archives of Sexual Behavior* 31.5: 413–9.

Frederick, R. J. 2009. *Living Like You Mean It: Use the Wisdom and Power of Your Emotions to Get the Life You Really Want.* San Francisco, CA: Jossey-Bass.

Friedman, M. S., M. P. Marshal, R. Stall, J. Cheong, and E. R. Wright. 2008. "Gay-related Development, Early Abuse and Adult Health Outcomes Among Gay Males." *AIDS and Behavior* 12: 891–902.

Gottman, J. M. 1999. *The Marriage Clinic: A Scientifically-Based Marital Therapy.* New York, NY: W. W. Norton & Company Inc.

Greenan, D. E. and G. Tunnell. 2003. *Couple Therapy With Gay Men.* New York, NY: The Guilford Press.

Iasenza, S. 2010. "What Is Queer About Sex?: Expanding Sexual Frames in Theory and Practice." *Family Process* 49 (3): 291–308.

Lehrer, J. 2010. *How We Decide.* New York, NY: First Mariner Books.

Morin, J. 1995. *The Erotic Mind: Unlocking the Inner Sources of Sexual Passion and Fulfillment.* New York, NY: HarperCollins Publishers.

Morrow, D. F. 2004. "Social Work Practice With Gay, Lesbian, Bisexual, and Transgender Adolescents." *Families in Society* 85 (1): 91–99.

Parsons, J. T., T. J. Starks, S. DuBois, C. Grov, and S. A. Golub. 2013. "Alternatives to Monogamy Among Gay Male Couples in a Community Survey: Implications for Mental Health and Sexual Risk." *Archives of Sexual Behavior* 42: 303–312.

Sanchez, F. J., and E. Vilan. 2012. "Straight-Acting Gays: The Relationship Between Masculine Consciousness, Anti-Effeminacy, and Negative Gay Identity." *Archives of Sexual Behavior* 41: 111–119.

Shilo, G., and R. Savaya. 2011. "Effects of Family and Friend Support on LGB Youths' Mental Health and Sexual Orientation Milestones." *Family Relations* 60 (3): 318–330.

Siegel, D. J. 2011. *Mindsight: The New Science of Personal Transformation.* New York, NY: Bantam Books.

Tatkin, S. 2011. *Wired for Love: How Understanding Your Partner's Brain and Attachment Style Can Help You Defuse Conflict and Build a Secure Relationship.* Oakland, CA: New Harbinger Publications, Inc.

Weber, G. N. 2008. "Using to Numb the Pain: Substance Use and Abuse Among Lesbian, Gay, and Bisexual Individuals." *Journal of Mental Health Counseling* 30 (1): 31–48.

Weber-Gilmore, G., S. Rose, and R. Rubinstein. 2011. "The Impact of Internalized Homophobia on Outness for Lesbian, Gay, and Bisexual Individuals." *The Professional Counselor* 1 (3): 163–175.

Made in United States
North Haven, CT
01 November 2025